ALSO BY BRET LOTT

Before We Get Started

Ballantine Books 🏛 New York

Before We Get Started

A PRACTICAL MEMOIR
OF THE WRITER'S LIFE

Bret Lott

Published in the United States by Ballantine Books, an
imprint of The Random House Publishing Group, a division
of Random House, Inc., New York.

Ballantine and colophon are registered trademarks of
Random House, Inc.

Grateful acknowledgment is made to the following for
permission to reprint previously published materials:

*Atria Books, an imprint of Simon & Schuster Adult Publishing
Group:* Excerpt from *Reed's Beach* by Bret Lott. Copyright ©
1993 by Bret Lott. Reprinted by permission of Atria Books,
an imprint of Simon & Schuster Adult Publishing Group,
New York.

An excerpt appears in this work from *A Stranger's House* by
Bret Lott, copyright © 1987 by Bret Lott (New York: Viking,
a division of Penguin Group [USA], Inc., 1987).

Library of Congress Cataloging-in-Publication Data

Lott, Bret.
Before we get started: on writing / Bret Lott.
p.   cm.
ISBN 0-345-47817-7 (pbk.)
1. Lott, Bret.   2. Novelists, American—20th century—
Biography.   3. English teachers—United States—Biography.
4. Editors—United States—Biography.   5. Lott, Bret—
Authorship.   6. Authorship.   I. Title.

PS3562.O784Z463 2005
813'.54—dc22   2004056802
[B]

Printed in the United States of America

Ballantine Books website address: www.ballantinebooks.com

9 8 7 6 5 4 3 2 1

First Edition

Text design by Simon M. Sullivan

For my students

Of making many books there is no end,
and much study wearies the body.

—ECCLESIASTES 12:12

Stare. It is the way to educate your eye, and more.
Stare, pry, listen, eavesdrop.
Die knowing something. You are not here long.

—WALKER EVANS

Contents

Before We Get Started

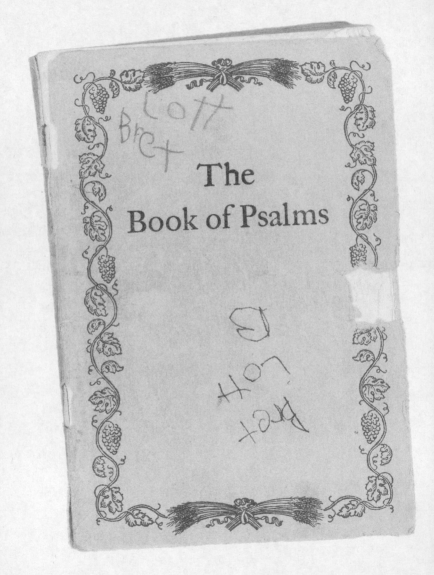

The
Book of Psalms

Genesis

●●●

I am sitting in the sanctuary, a few rows from the front, to my left my mom and dad, my little brother, Timmy, in Mom's lap and sleeping, to my right my older brother, Brad. Brad and I have just received these thin blue books, every kid in the service passed a brand-new copy by men in gray or black suits standing at either end of the pews, stacks of these books in hand.

The blue paper cover is bordered with green grapevines, tendrils working up and down either side with bunches of grapes here and there; at the top and bottom of the cover those tendrils meet sheaves of wheat in the same green ink.

The pastor says it is the book of *somms,* and I wonder what that is, look at the words in black ink centered a little high on the cover. I sound out the words to myself, *The . . . Book . . . of,* and stop.

P-S-A-L-M-S. How does that, I wonder, spell out *Somms*?

But even if I don't understand, this is the first Bible—or

piece of it—I have ever gotten, and I don't want to lose this book. I want to keep it.

So I take one of the nubby pencils from the back of the pew in front of me, nestled in its tiny wooden hole beside the wooden shelf where attendance forms are kept, and beside the larger holes where the tiny glass cups are placed once we've emptied them of grape juice.

And I begin, for the first time in my life, to write my name by myself.

I start at the upper-left-hand corner, just below the border, but the first word trails off, falls toward that centered title in black as though that title is a magnet, the letters I make iron filings. They fall that way because there are no lines for me to balance them upon, as I am able to do with the paper given me by my kindergarten teacher, Mrs. Pasley.

I finish that first word, feel in my hand the cramp of so much strenuous, focused work, and hold the book away from me, look at it while the pastor rolls on.

There is no place for the second word, I see, the last letter of my first name too near the first of the title.

This is a problem. I know the second word must follow the first on the same line, a little space needed between them. Mrs. Pasley would not approve. This is a problem.

But there is space above my name due to its falling away, a wedge of blue field that might, if I am careful enough, be able to hold that second word, and I write, work out the riddle of letters without lines, letters that will line up to mark this book as mine, and mine only.

Then I am finished, and here is my name. Me.

The first time I have ever written my name myself, alone.

Later, on the way home, my older brother, Brad, will look at the book, say, "Lott Bret. Who's that?" and laugh at my ill-spaced effort. Later still I will write my name again on the cover, this time with a blue pen and holding the book upside down. The words will be a little more jaunty, full of themselves and the confidence of a kid who knows how to write his name, no problem at all. Beneath this second round, though, will be the lone letter *B*, a practice swing at making that capital letter as good as I can make it.

Later, I will be baptized into the church at age fourteen, a ritual it will seem to me is the right thing to do.

Later still, in college, I will be born again, as Christ instructed Nicodemus.

And later even still, I will have written entire books of my own, created lives out of the whole cloth of the imagination. I will have created, and created in my name.

But on this Sunday, the pastor still rolling on, these two words themselves are enough.

Only a kid's scrawl. My own small imitation of God.

• •

Let me begin this book on the nature and aim of words by saying that I won't be talking about those glamour words we all get
to use now and again, the ones that set our pride spinning at our
actually using in a sentence. *Abrogate* was one of those words I
used that, once I'd actually employed it correctly in a sentence,
made me lean back and put my hands behind my head, kick my
feet up on the desk, and beam at my intelligence. Another one I
love is the word *limn*, which I've used a number of times for
what I hope was good effect. Once, in a review of a perfectly
dreadful novel that centered on hidden incestuous relationships, I had the great good fortune of putting together the phrase
"the most Byzantine jamboree of family flesh possible." That was
a glorious occasion, I remember, and I remember, too, me smiling at the monitor for a good five minutes about that. *Byzantine
jamboree.* That was fun.

But I won't be talking about those words here. The kind of

words I'm talking about are those trench-warfare words, those grunt-work words we oftentimes don't give a second thought because we traffic in them day in and day out, truck them in and off-load them like they were so many yards of gravel being used to rough-pave the road for the brilliant parade of paper floats our ideas and ambitions and intellect will be once this story is done.

Byzantine jamboree. Man, that was fun.

No. I'll be talking about *a, the,* and *this.* Those few small words we couldn't care less about because they are, like the poor, always with us.

But before I begin holding forth on even that much—those three numbingly nondescript syllables that together only use up three vowels and three consonants—I need to tell you about how I used to live behind a guy who used the term *no-brainer* way too often. He was a doctor—a gastroenterologist—and because doctors know everything precisely because they are doctors, it was never any surprise to me that everything he encountered was a "no-brainer."

And because he used it so often in our everyday exchanges— from the "no-brainer" it was for him to buy a two-year-old Lexus instead of a new one, to the "no-brainer" it was deciding to scope a patient complaining of blood in his phlegm—slowly the term crept into my own lexicon, until for a while I was walking around saying it just as much as he was. It's a fun term, I found out, infectious for its sharp little shorthand expressing your own acumen and eloquence at once.

"Can I get a transverse Mohawk?" my older son, Zeb, once asked me. Really.

"That's a no-brainer," I told him. Meaning, I hoped he understood, no.

"That's a no-brainer," I said when Jacob asked if he could ride his bike alone to Wendy's for lunch one Saturday back when he was in the third or fourth grade. He'd have to cross Highway 17 where Mathis Ferry Road intersected it, six lanes without a crosswalk.

But I've since kicked the habit—or almost. Because, finally, I hate that term. There's something about it that smacks of condescension, something in it that implies everyone else is an idiot who can't assess and discuss things as quickly and accurately as you.

Which leads to how I'd like to begin this book: with a moment a few semesters ago when I almost blurted out, "That's a no-brainer," to a student in class.

This was toward the beginning of things, during the critique of one of the first student stories, all of us doing the old workshop shuffle: what you like, what you don't, what works, what doesn't, what's at stake, what's missing, blah blah blah, all in the hopes not just to put a Band-Aid on the story at hand but to try to speak of the larger notion of writing fiction. There was a particular point I wanted to make about the way the student used a noun and its synonyms, and how its usage called into question the verisimilitude of the entire story, because it called into question the authority of the writer herself.

Within one page of a story told in the first person, the narrator had referred to her mother as her *mom,* her *momma,* and her *mother.* I pointed this out to the class as being a matter of consistency of both point of view and of voice—that is, in order to get a first-person narrator nailed down so that the reader can begin to get to know the character and thereby come to whatever experience the story might offer, the writer needs to use language consistently, in this case decide whether the narrator calls her mother "mom," "momma," or "mother." Of course there are lots of different considerations that go into making such a blanket statement: What if the narrator is fragmented herself, is unreliable and so does not in fact know any kind of consistency in her own voice? What if her mother is to her three persons at once, a kind of matriarchal holy trinity? What if she calls her "momma" in dialogue, but thinks of her as "mother" when relating the story here on the page? What if what if what if? Certainly extenuating, qualifying circumstances are always at work. But the story we were reading carried with it none of those free passes to arguing with the teacher.

I made this point about the noun and its usage, and made it pretty well, I thought. Hey, I'd been doing this for a long time. I'd made this little speech enough times before. They're getting it, I thought.

And then I glanced to my left to see a student with her nose wrinkled up, as though smelling something false. She wasn't one of those kinds of belligerent students, either, those sorts who think they know something going in and so rebut everything that comes out of your mouth in order to hold together the sad and tattered last shreds of the nomad's tent their understanding of writing has become. Those students you hope and pray will not darken your door because when they do, the semester can stretch out before you like the Hundred Years' War. No, she was a fine writer, seemed sensible, and so I asked her, "What's wrong?"

"I don't see why that matters," she said, and shrugged, still with her nose wrinkled up.

This was when I very nearly said, "That's a no-brainer." Instead, I caught myself, and went on to beat her and the rest of the class about the ears with the blunt instrument of my further instruction, as I am wont to do when somebody doesn't get what I want them to get.

I'm going to pause a moment or two here to quote a little piece of a lecture I gave during the first residency I spent teaching in the low-residency M.F.A. program at Vermont College, back in 1994, this in the hopes of illuminating why this particular moment in my teaching life—an undergrad's pooh-poohing my point about nouns—was one that carried a bit more weight than it might otherwise seem.

The lecture was on the architecture of Jayne Anne Phillips's *Machine Dreams.* But the section I'm going to quote doesn't have anything to do with her book; instead, it's a passage I hope will relate the sort of self-deluding snobbery bred by looking at words as though their examination one by one were beneath us. Or at least beneath me.

When I was in grad school at UMass Amherst I took a seminar in Virginia Woolf from Lee Edwards. There were about ten or eleven of us in there, and it just so happened that that semester there was a centennial celebration of Woolf's birthday down at Pembroke, a three-day shindig at which plenty of papers would be presented on what was becoming, in no small part due to Lee Edwards's teaching capabilities, our favorite writer. We decided to go down there for a day of the festivities, and piled in two cars, drove all the way to Providence. We got lost once in town, finally found the right building, and walked in, all of us, on a panel already in progress. I don't remember who the heck the presenter was talking up there, but it soon became obvious to each of us that we had no clue what she was saying, only that it had to do with *The Waves*. When she finished, the crowded room applauded enthusiastically and we all sort of looked at one another, shrugged.

The next presenter stood and began reading her own paper, this one about the use of personal pronouns in *To the Lighthouse*.

That was when we stood as a group, and filed out. Once in the hallway, we shook our heads, perplexed at the lifeblood being sucked out of books we loved happening just inside the closed doors behind us. We found a pub down one or another street, and all sat at a table, and talked about the books we'd been reading for class, why we loved them, why not. Then, disillusioned at the proceedings but glad for each other's company, all that talk, we piled back in the cars, drove on home to western Mass.

The talk, of course, let me and each of the others simply come to know more fully those books, and how and why and when they moved our hearts. Hearts moving, by the way, the reason any of us ought to write.

Well, okay. I'll give myself that last line. It seems true enough, these many years later, that moving the heart is the reason we ought to write. But I can't help but think how smug I sounded, and how unwilling to learn I was, not just back in 1983 when we did all that, but as near to now in my own history as when I gave that lecture, in 1994. Because the longer I write—and this is the one sure thing I know about writing—

the harder it gets, and the more I hold close the truth that I know nothing.

I can't help but think of how smug I was to very nearly blurt out to that student, "That's a no-brainer."

Because, if you want to write, there really is no such thing as a no-brainer. Flannery O'Connor wrote, "There's a grain of stupidity that the writer of fiction can hardly do without, and this is the quality of having to stare, of not getting the point at once." I think what she's saying is that if one begins to see the world and its dilemmas and desires and questions and heartbreaks and, yes, noun forms as being no-brainers, one has begun to lose the necessary wonder at and reverence for what is eternally unfolding around us that it takes to be one "upon whom nothing is lost," as Henry James exhorted writers to be.

Wonder and *reverence*, I want to say before I get started, are the twin dynamos that generate the art of writing.

To look at something without wonder and reverence—to see things as being no-brainers—is to dismiss *deliberation;* dismissing deliberation eliminates the possibility for *reflection;* to eliminate reflection is simply and fully and sadly to reject the possibility of *discovery.* Of course the difference between *a* and *the* and *this* is a vast one. Of course words matter. Of course we must choose carefully.

But why is there such a vast difference? And given the endless valley of bones the same old words used again and again and again by writers far superior to ourselves truly is, we writers no more than buzzards picking over the same words used by Faulkner and Melville and O'Connor and Hawthorne and Welty and Baldwin and all of them—given all those words, and our pitiful little attempts at recycling them in the hopes we might create our own Holden Caulfields or Lily Briscoes or Boo Rad-leys, attempts that most often result not in literature but in the same sort of recycling that goes on in the lower intestines of those same buzzards—well, given the same words as always, why must we be so careful?

Why do words matter so?

And in thinking about the why, I have been led deeper and deeper into this whole thing called writing, and deeper and deeper into what it means to be a writer altogether, until I have arrived here, now, writing this thing down for you and me both, discovering as I sit here that there is, finally, too much to say about this topic. Before I get started here, I want to say that everything—everything—regarding writing gets right down to the difference between *a* and *the* and *this*. The more I think about it the more I am convinced that there really is *nothing else* to talk about.

Because all things are informed by the word one writes next, and the one after that, and the one after that. All things come down to the difference between one word and another. All things: point of view, tone, characterization, body language, set-ting, dialogue, theme, symbols.

Meaning.

Let me start with saying the word means everything.

But first, let's get back to *mom, momma,* and *mother.*

Here I was, making a case for the importance of the use of noun forms in a story, when in my own life I'd walked out of such a talk on one of my favorite writers because I in my ig-norance believed myself to be superior, to be above these mat-ters of pronouns, talk of which I asserted was sucking out the lifeblood of the work of Virginia Woolf, when I in my ignorance did not know that in fact the use of the personal pronouns was the lifeblood itself. The use of the word is the lifeblood. All this brought home to me, the teacher, nearly twenty years later by a student story in which personal pronouns were used willy-nilly. Mom, or momma, or mother matters, and the wrinkling of a nose by an undergrad sniffing out the ponderous notion of such a statement reminded me of none other than me, standing and filing out of a lecture hall at Pembroke with a disdainful posse of young writers bent on making certain they—we—I—knew what was important about writing: bar talk. Not the use of pronouns.

And it just so happened that in that particular class meeting we had just finished talking about "Kiss Away," a Charles Baxter story from the collection *Believers,* one of the standards I use for my classes. For some reason there came to me a sentence from that story that exhibited precisely the importance of what I mean when I say the difference is vast between *the* and *a* and *this.*

Here's the sentence: "She had worn a rather formal white ruffled blouse with the palm tree pin, and a dark blue suit, and she had a semi-matching blue purse, at the sight of which Walton had announced that Jodie had 'starched notions of elegance,' a phrase he didn't care to explain."

The sentence seems innocuous enough in and of itself, and describes what she has worn to her first job interview since meeting Walton, a strange and sort of mystic character she spots from the sleeping porch of the house she's living in at the beginning of the story. It is my hope you have read or will read the story, and so I won't say much more about this or any of the other stories I will mention in terms of intricacies of plot. Suffice it to say she has dwelt inside a kind of lethargic sense of self that, until meeting Walton, seemed destined for paralysis.

Then here is this word *the* before the words *palm tree pin*.

The rest of her attire here is brought to us courtesy of the lonely and shivering indefinite article *a*, but the palm tree pin is delivered by the confident, even cocksure definite article *the*.

Here, in this single word, is the fulcrum of the story, the moment in which the story takes its turn for its fruition, its revelation, its meaning. We have neither seen the palm tree pin before this nor see it again afterward, yet in her selecting the palm tree pin, an object made intimate by its being labeled with the definite article and not the indefinite, we see that in fact there is something deeply at stake in her choosing to get a job, or at least choosing to get out of the house in order to pursue one. The palm tree pin signals us that the pin has some kind of importance to Jodie and hence is a sign of hope in her heart, however small, that her life will improve.

She doesn't get that job. She doesn't get the next, or the next, but finally lands one. Getting a job is not the key to the story, and her gainful employment is not what finally brings her to love and security in the midst of a dangerous world, the same world, in fact, she inhabits at the beginning of the story.

But it is the *the* here that ushers in the security she finds only after making herself vulnerable to an indefinite article of a world, that cold and anonymous world she has inhabited just before the *the* appears.

This story, I submit, relies on *the*.

I talked to Mr. Baxter just now—Friday, June 23, 2000, at 5:35 P.M.—to see if I was on the right track in all this. He is my favorite living writer, I do not hesitate to say, and has been a friend for many years—I even had the privilege of shoveling his driveway of snow one February afternoon while I was a guest at his house, just so I could impress my readers in some future essay by writing, "I shoveled Charlie Baxter's driveway of snow one February afternoon"—and so I figured I would go to the source, just in case I was making too much of this all. I shot the breeze with him for a while, then presented to him what I have here, to which he responded, "Whatever you tell those people, you tell them I said, 'Bret, my friend, you are right as rain.' " So there.

But he also went on, because in fact understanding words and their meanings does matter to writers, to say that when he wrote that sentence he was using the pin "as a means to show her increasing identification with the objects of her own life, and so her increasing identification with herself in light of this new relationship with Walton." That is, in the pin she is coming to see herself, to know herself again. She is coming to life.

So, you may be wondering, what does this example have to do with my assertion that everything in a story has to do with the difference between *a* and *the* and *this*? To begin with, there is plot: this day she chooses a pin that has meaning to her, and in choosing that pin she is making herself vulnerable to defeat, to not getting a job, but she goes forward regardless; as for character development, she is increasingly identifying herself in relationship to the objects she owns, thereby showing us the growth in her character; as for how this informs point of view, because this word *the* carries no associations with it that would reveal the pin's actual history to us—where she got it and how—we see we are so deeply embedded in her point of view that in fact there is no need for associations. Just as when one walks into one's bedroom and looks at the dresser for the keys or tube of Chap Stick or half-roll of cherry Life Savers before walking out of the house, one doesn't in that moment necessarily stand in silent pontification upon the memories and histories all the objects littered across the dresser might elicit at some other point. We are instead in her point of view, and in deep: this pin means something.

I could have gone on with that story for the rest of the class period, but there came to me, in the blessed way things sometimes come to teachers in the trench of fighting the good fight getting your students to see can and always will be, the fact we'd just recently read Flannery O'Connor's story "A Good Man Is Hard to Find," and—and you can believe or not believe this came to me, too—a usage of the indefinite article *a* that, I believe, serves as a fulcrum as well. There's a place in the story, I remembered, where that single letter exists as a dagger to the base of the spine in what it shows not only of the reality of death, but also a transcendence—or, depending on your interpretation, debasement—of the grandmother's soul.

This is one of my favorite stories ever; its presence is never far from mind whenever I'm talking about short stories. There is contained in it humor, tragedy, physical comedy and the play of words, notions of Grace and Jesus and the stark truth of how close we all are to our own mortality not just of body, but more importantly of soul.

But before I got to all that with this group of young writers impatient to get back to the student's story being critiqued, and with me fully aware of the necessary breach of protocol leaving a story splayed open there in the middle of the room, I pointed out a few images, and the point of view taking them in.

The first moment occurs immediately after the accident precipitated by the grandmother's cat erupting from the basket, where she has secreted it away. To draw attention away from the fact this whole damn thing is all her fault, the grandmother says, "I believe I have an injured organ." Then O'Connor writes, "Bailey's teeth were clattering. He had on a yellow sport shirt with bright blue parrots designed in it and his face was as yellow as the shirt."

Here we have, pretty late in the story, the first mention of this ghastly yellow shirt, its color inextricably tied to the fear and anger and perplexity and simple surprise of adrenaline of this moment. The second mention comes after the grandmother, who can't keep her mouth shut, identifies The Misfit, thereby making it inevitable that she and the rest of the family will be killed.

O'Connor writes, " 'Listen,' Bailey began, 'we're in a terrible predicament! Nobody realizes what this is,' and his voice cracked. His eyes were as blue and intense as the parrots in his shirt and he remained perfectly still."

Here we are brought, through the shirt, not anger or exasperation, but dead, paralyzed, panicked fear, fear so deep and so intense that the head of the household cannot finish his sentence. He knows what is coming. He knows.

A few lines later arrive the grandmother's last moments of pleading lucidity in the world she inhabits before what will surely come to pass, a world shattered by the single pistol shot in the woods followed closely by another, a world of sin and depravity she thinks will be solved by the simple act of prayer.

But The Misfit will have none of it, and then this:

Bobby Lee and Hiram came ambling back from the woods. Bobby Lee was dragging a yellow shirt with bright blue parrots in it.

"Throw me that shirt, Bobby Lee," The Misfit said. The shirt came flying at him and landed on his shoulder and he put it on. The grandmother couldn't name what the shirt reminded her of.

A yellow shirt.

That single letter *a* serves double duty here. In the first place, the chilling effect of its being unnamed and unknown—it is only a shirt—when in reality it was worn by her son only moments before, serves, I hold, as that dagger at the base of the spine: prior to this moment the violence of this all has existed first in the abstract—the escaped convicts arrive, are identified, words are passed by the son as to the possibility of what might happen, offstage the pistol reports shout from the woods—only to have that violence brought front and center, no argument or doubt or relief from its impending presence in the grandmother's life about it: her son's shirt is now a shirt. No one's.

This letter *a* also reveals her character in that we see this all through her eyes, through her sensibilities, the indefinite article illuminating who she has become in this moment that tests, finally and utterly, her faith in and understanding of Grace. There is no longer any recognition, no longer any evidence before her of her son's life. And here is where I believe that transcendence—or debasement—of her soul occurs: she now replaces her son with The Misfit himself.

All this pinnable on that letter *a*.

—

And finally, in this particular classroom on this particular day at the end of what had seemed a particularly unremarkable workshop, I remembered yet one more instance of the importance of these small words, this from another story we had all read: Raymond Carver's "Where I'm Calling From."

I could have spent that entire long afternoon simply talking about the craft of this story, the way the point-of-view character—never named—tells J.P.'s story as though inhabiting it were a means to avoid the reality of his own sorry life. I could have talked, too, about the use of the single personal pronoun *me,* uttered only three times in the story.

The word appears twice near the end of the story, when the narrator, still and always nameless, finally engages himself in a memory—a good one—from his past life, a moment when, sober and naked, he stands before the landlord outside his bedroom of a Sunday morning, the landlord setting out to paint the house before the day gets too hot, the narrator's wife laughing and calling the narrator back to bed. Carver writes, "And at that minute a wave of happiness comes over me that I'm not him—that I'm me and that I'm inside this bedroom with my wife." This usage of the word *me* is a precursor to the last word of the story, when the nameless narrator finally knows who he is: "It's me," he says, and lays claim to his own life, the reality of it and the need for his own moving, however tentatively, out into it. He calls neither his girlfriend nor his wife, please note. He doesn't actually do anything here. He only recognizes himself.

But there is also an intriguing and, again, fulcrumatic, if I may invent such a word, use of one of those grunt-work words I've been talking about, this time the word *this.*

"Imagine this kid!" the narrator exhorts us at one point in

the story in describing the loudmouth son of his girlfriend. That word *this* carries with it no value whatsoever, the word existing in this context and throughout the story only as a kind of unceremonious shorthand adjective for virtually everything and everyone in the story, from Roxy who "plants this kiss" on his lips to the fact of Tiny's seizures haunting his own waking life with the possibility of lost control: "So every time this little flitter starts up anywhere, I draw some breath and wait to find myself on my back, looking up, somebody's fingers in my mouth."

Yet in that same last paragraph as the narrator's declaration of identity, there is a strange and wonderful turn from the loose change that word *this* is used for throughout, when suddenly, in identifying himself, the narrator says, "There's no way to make a joke out of this."

Suddenly and without warning, the familiar inarticulate adjective becomes the entire noun of his present life, a noun—a life—that is unforeseeable at this particular moment of light, but which is a noun nonetheless. The word *this* precipitates, then, his ability simply to lay claim to being *me,* and moving forward into whatever gray world he sees he has no choice but to move into next.

This is the *me* of who he is *now.*

And so, for all these reasons, I'd like to start this book with the suggestion we be careful with the word, no matter how "small." I propose that in caring for the word, in all its light and texture and density and purpose, we see ourselves as the servants to the word we are called to be as writers. I would like to begin by suggesting that even the single letter *a* is worthy of our carrying, through the long and arduous and fulfilling and ill-attended parade our writing lives will be, as though it were a golden crown on a tufted velvet pillow, and not so many yards of gravel dumped on a roadbed. Our ideas, our ambitions, our intellect truly are, after all, nothing more than paper floats. The word came before us, and will live on after us, whether that word be a single timorous letter or a polysyllabic fiesta.

But should the sheer weight even the word *a* can carry daunt us? Should we now hold up each use of every word to the cold light of all of literature before we even put it to pen, or at least commit it to the electronic impulses trafficking in the yes-and-no language of our computers, 1, 0, 1, 0, 1?

Well, 1, and 0. Yes, and no.

Because though I have pointed out these instances of what might seem micromanagement of the word by the author, I do not for an instant believe that these writers spent much time in the moment of passion and joy and sorrow and opacity and understanding that is the moment of creation. I may be wrong, but I am willing to venture that it was through their faith in the indescribable and unteachable moment of inspiration—and by this I mean both that moment of divine guidance or influence exerted directly on the mind and soul of humankind, and the act of drawing air into the lungs—that these writers proceeded, as carefully and thoughtlessly as we each of us breathe in and breathe out, with the words chosen, seeing those characters they had created no longer through a glass darkly, but in the firm and brilliant light of truth. They saw these characters in their own moments of truth, and let reach the page the smallest scratches of meaningful ink: *a, the, this.*

Regardless to whom one may ascribe those moments of inspiration, inspiration they will be, and unteachable they will remain.

But the weight of words should not—cannot—be reason enough to cease carrying them. Nor should the fact they have been used, and used better, by so many great writers paralyze us. Faced with that endless valley of bones we have available to us, we must do what Ezekiel did: we must bring those bones to life. Ezekiel's vision can teach us a lot about writing, though I've never seen it on any creative writing course's reading list. Here are his words:

> The hand of the Lord came upon me and brought me out in the Spirit of the Lord, and set me down in the midst of the valley; and it was full of bones. Then He caused me to pass by them all around, and behold, there were very many in the open valley; and indeed they were very dry. And He said to me, "Son of man, can these bones live?" So I answered, "O Lord God, You know." Again He said to me, "Prophesy to these bones, and say to them, 'O dry bones, hear the word of the Lord! Thus says the Lord God to these bones: "Surely I will cause breath to enter into you, and you shall live. I will put sinews on you and bring flesh upon you, cover you with skin and put breath in you; and you shall live. Then you shall know that I am the Lord." ' " So I prophesied as I was commanded; and as I prophesied, there was a noise, and suddenly a rattling; and the bones came together, bone to bone. Indeed, as I looked, the sinews and the flesh came upon them, and the skin covered them over; but there was no breath in them. Also He said to me, "Prophesy to the breath, prophesy, son of man, and say to the breath, 'Thus says the Lord God: "Come from the four winds, O breath, and breathe

on these slain, that they may live." ' " So I prophesied as He commanded me, and breath came into them, and they lived, and stood upon their feet, an exceedingly great army. Then He said to me, "Son of man, these bones are the whole house of Israel. They indeed say, 'Our bones are dry, our hope is lost, and we ourselves are cut off!' Therefore prophesy and say to them, 'Thus says the Lord God: "Behold, O My people, I will open your graves and cause you to come up from your graves, and bring you into the land of Israel. Then you shall know that I am the Lord, when I have opened your graves, O My people, and brought you up from your graves. I will put My Spirit in you, and you shall live, and I will place you in your own land. Then you shall know that I, the Lord, have spoken it and performed it," says the Lord.' "

One can only imagine Ezekiel standing there and being questioned by God as to God's power, and I don't think it would be too far from the truth to imagine that Ezekiel, knees trembling before the despair of so many bones and God breathing down his neck for an answer, thought fleetingly, dangerously, *There's no way. Bones to life? Nope.*

But it is a testament to his wisdom, and I think perhaps an indictment of his skepticism as well, that his answer is one of reflection: "O Lord God, You know." He doesn't say, *You bet.* He doesn't say, *Don't think so.* He leaves it to God, and then proceeds—and here is the most important moment—*to speak the prophecy he has been called to speak,* whether he believes it or not, and not knowing as well what that prophecy means. He speaks, because he has been called to, and not because he knows what will be the outcome.

And then these dry bones come to life.

And then, in the writer's answer to whatever has called him to write, and in his willingness to look at each word with fear and trepidation coupled with faith that speaking it will be an act in obedience to what has called him to speak it, those words will line up, will breathe, will become the vast army of sentences that will take up residence in the new Israel every story, novel, essay, and poem ought to be.

Finally, I'd like to start this book by saying that in the beginning was the Word, and that in the original Greek the Gospel of John was written in, the word *Word* was *logos,* which translated also means reason.

The old cliché is that, in the best scenario a teacher can encounter, the teacher will learn from the student. That's a no-brainer, I want to say before I get started. And such was the case on an otherwise procedural day in an undergrad creative writing class when a sensible student wrinkled her nose at an assertion I made.

I want to begin by saying words matter, so pick them carefully.

So. Let's begin.

Why Write, Anyway?

If there's one truth that comes out of your writing education, one single nugget of plain truth you can walk away with, it will be this: you're on your own.

Despite the fact we are as human beings pattern makers, beings who find it necessary to believe that there are right and wrong ways to do things, quicker and easier paths through the world jungle we all inhabit, it just ain't so. Learning to write—how-to—is a desperately idiosyncratic, eccentric, single-souled lifelong quest, a journey you have to make alone. Anyone who pretends otherwise is a crock.

But we have been driven to be here, driven to do what we are doing for one reason and another, for better and worse. Which prompts me to ask the big ugly question: why write, anyway?

And now that I have asked this question, the story of my own why is, I see, the only thing I know. I am the owner of only one story, my own, and for that reason must give it back to you, coupled with a number of quotes from vastly superior writers who have wandered through precisely this terrain long before I ever did, my story and their words offered up to you all in the hopes some or any of this might help illuminate and galvanize the why of which only you are the owner. So here goes:

In the summer of 1994, I lost my publisher, Pocket Books, a division of Simon & Schuster, as the sales figures for *Reed's Beach,* my latest novel, sucked. Never mind the reviews for the book, or the sales figures and reviews for the previous novel, *Jewel.* Never mind, as well, the reviews or sales of any of my three books prior to that. My editor had already bought the next two books after *Reed's Beach,* a story collection and a memoir, but then took maternity leave. While she was gone, the publisher left, a new one brought in. This new publisher took one look at my sales figures and handed back to my editor the books, who then handed them back to my agent. Then my editor called me to tell me the news. It was a call I will not forget, especially this line, which I have since committed to memory, so stinging was the truth my newly former editor uttered: "Bret," she said, "the problem with your literary career is that you're white, male, and don't make good copy for *People* magazine." Guilty on all three counts.

Six months before this I had begun working on my next novel, when here were returned the next two books, complete and already paid for. I know, I know; everybody should have such problems. Here's a guy who had already published four books, and now he's moaning. Everybody should have such problems.

Regardless of this truth—who was I to complain?—I am a writer of books. This is what I do, and I was still working on a new novel, one whose future it had seemed was assured. I had led up to that time a charmed—I prefer blessed—publishing life: my first novel came out from Viking when I was twenty-eight, and was followed the next year by the second novel, the next year by a story collection, all with Viking. Two years later came *Jewel,* a year and a half after that *Reed's Beach,* both from Pocket Books. Except for the first one, *The Man Who Owned Vermont,* which was turned down twelve times before being bought by Viking, each book was written with the knowledge that someone wanted it, that editors were waiting for it.

Which was something of the belief I held going into the next one, the one I was working on when these other two came back. I had been seduced—I am willing to admit—into believing I had a publishing life, that people were waiting for the next book, that I was secure. And this, of course, was my folly, and what sent me into the tailspin I experienced most of the next two and a half years.

I ended up having writer's block, though I have never claimed an actual belief in that. I kept telling myself that I just wasn't writing, while all the time growing more glum, more sullen. I worked bit by bit on the next novel, while my agent tried to sell the memoir—the story collection came back to me, gathered dust on my desk, as no one in New York seemed remotely interested in these things.

It was then I had to begin to wrestle with this whole thing of my own why. Why was I writing, I wanted to know, when no one around me seemed at all interested in seeing the next? Why try to finish the next scene? Why try to write another essay? Why try to start up a new story?

The answers to these questions, of course, are as varied as there are people who write. John Braine wrote of this matter,

"You must remember that you yourself don't matter; only the work matters," while David Wagoner writes, "After all, you want to be remembered in life. And why should you be remembered if you don't do anything memorable?" And of course there's Flannery O'Connor's deceptively glib quote, when asked by an interviewer why she wrote: "Because I'm good at it." Unfortunately for me, the only answers I seemed able to come up with were ones that made me see in fact how shallow my expectations of it all had become: I wrote, it seemed, because I was being published, and had forgotten much of the good writing brings about, those parts of all this that go often unnoticed (at least by me) but which we are always told are the more noble reasons: to understand on your own your own story, the joy of finding just the right word, the depth of feeling one can only experience in creating real people out of nothing.

Who cares about those noble reasons, I was feeling once I'd been given the boot, and trying to write that next novel, when for the eight years prior to all this bad news I'd been writing—and publishing—like mad.

Things happened: six months later my agent sold the memoir—called *Fathers, Sons, and Brothers,* about my being any or all three at any given moment—to another publisher, Orchard, a children's book publisher that was expanding to include adult books as well. They paid for it, printed galleys, sent out catalogs with the book in it. Only then to cancel the adult line six months before the book was to come out. And meanwhile the layer of dust on the story collection grew thicker.

What was escaping me all this while, me still chipping away at the novel, and me with no heart in it whatsoever—I cannot tell you the number of times I moaned to my wife that I wanted to quit writing, that I could see myself just being a teacher of English and mowing the lawn on weekends, began even to long for that life—what was escaping me all this while were the elemental truths of writing, the ones one encounters only through the doing of it.

"If the writing can't be made as good as it is within us to make it, then why do it?" wrote Raymond Carver on his own why. "In the end, the satisfaction of having done our best, and the proof of that labor, is the one thing we can take into the grave."

And so the work went on, the novel slowly, slowly taking a shape, while elsewhere the business of writing took its own twists and turns: a friend of mine, Robin Hemley, published his collection of stories with a small but elegant press in North Carolina, John F. Blair; he suggested I send them my story collection, which I did, and which they then took, publishing it in the summer of 1996. But it was a matter of resignation that sent me to that press: New York was no longer interested in my work, as the memoir, once again on the block, continued to be sent around, being turned down time and again. Perhaps the most telling rejection of that book, and the one that hurt the most, came from the vice president of a major literary publishing house (I won't say who), whose entire editorial board voted to buy the book. In her letter to me clarifying why they did not buy it, the vice president explained that when she brought the manuscript to the marketing director for his take on the book, he said, "This is one of the most beautifully written books I can remember reading, but the essays are about such normal people, I have no idea how we would market this."

Marketing.

I moaned louder of my desire to do yardwork.

It must be noted here that the novel I was writing was a different kind, a mystery, I kept telling myself, though when my agent read parts of it she said, "It's not a mystery, but another Bret Lott book." Which is a compliment from her. Yet I was doing—trying to do—something new for me, an adventure, the next kind of book to write, one I wanted to write out of a sense of release from the novel prior to it, *Reed's Beach*, which is about the death of a child. While a grad student at the University of Massachusetts Amherst, I was fortunate enough to have been chosen to be in a creative writing workshop taught by James Baldwin. The class was made up of three students each from one of the Five Colleges (UMass Amherst, Amherst, Smith, Mount Holyoke, and Hampshire), and though Mr. Baldwin proved to be not much of a teacher of workshops—he simply seemed unable to tell us how to write a good story or what was wrong with our own—I still got one of the best pockets of education I have ever received. It consisted of this: he simply spoke of art, of its importance, its relevance, its necessity. He spoke of the artist, and the need to write, the need to keep writing, writing no matter what. And when on the last day of the class we had a party at a fellow student's apartment, I cornered Mr. Baldwin in the way eager grad students sometimes do with teachers they believe can give them something to keep. I asked him point-blank, "Now that we're done with this class, what can you tell me?"

He looked at me, smiled, and said, "Once you know how to do one thing, move on to the next."

Here I was, employing that truth in my own writing life with this next novel, a mystery. I wanted to have fun with this next book, to write something with plot, with things happening, as it seemed most of my novels' plotlines consisted of a husband and wife standing in a kitchen, thinking about things. *Reed's Beach* was by no means the feel-good book of the summer. And still I kept writing and not writing, and still I kept wondering why, even though I was doing what Mr. Baldwin had taught me to do.

And yet Mr. Baldwin's words elsewhere also came to haunt me, to dog me and vex me with their truth yet again: "People pay for what they do," he wrote, "and still more, for what they have allowed themselves to become. And they pay for it simply: by the lives they lead." For me, as I said above, the validation of all this had become the publishing of it, and even though the story collection had been bought, it had been bought by a press outside New York, and that damned memoir was still going around. The life I was leading was a life that let the tail wag the dog: publishing was my preoccupation, and not writing.

This was when the dangerous end of things began: I started thinking it was the work. That the writing itself was bad, and so I stopped work on the new novel, beginning to convince myself that indeed I had perhaps lost the confidence necessary to make language new, lost the trust in myself to step into the void of the blank page and believe I could create. "A writer's successes," John Gardner wrote, "bring him more than praise, publication, or money: they also help him toward confidence. With each success, writers, like stunt riders and ballet dancers, learn to dare more." I was beginning to lose that confidence, what Richard Hugo called a kind of arrogance. "To write you must have a streak of arrogance," he wrote. "By arrogance I mean that when you are writing you must assume that the next thing you put down belongs not for reasons of logic, good sense, or narrative development, but because you put it there."

Again, Gardner wrote, "In order to be a good novelist, what a writer needs most is an almost demonic compulsiveness . . . [which] can kill as easily as it can save. The true novelist must be at once driven and indifferent. Drivenness helps only if it forces the writer not to suicide but to the making of works of art, allowing him indifference to whether or not the novel sells, whether or not it's appreciated."

I had begun to lose that indifference, begun, in fact, to believe in the machine.

William Stafford wrote, "Becoming a writer is just partly the learning of tricks and processes of language. Literature comes about by way of a behavior, a way of thinking, a tendency of mind and feeling. We can all learn technique and then improvise pieces of writing again and again, but without a certain security of character we cannot sustain the vision, the trajectory of significant creation: we can learn and know and still not understand. Perceiving the need for that security of character is not enough—you have to possess it, and it is a gift, or something like a gift. You can't earn it, or calculate how to get it. But it may come, when you enter the life of writing with patience and trust."

This loss of my own trust in myself, this deadening of my own gift by learning not to believe in that gift is the most dangerous end of things, as this is when what has driven you to write is short-circuited in a kind of literary suicide: one pulls the plug on oneself when one no longer believes, or places one's belief in that to which we are called to be indifferent: the publication. For none of us here ought to be writing so that we can see our name in print. If that is the case, then one need only write letters to the editor.

This belief in the machine, then, can and does lead to the denial of one's own heart, and the disavowing of what matters, finally, if one wants truly to write. Brenda Ueland, in her book *If You Want to Write,* writes of her own why: "At last I understood that writing was this: an impulse to share with other people a feeling or truth that I myself had. Not to preach to them, but to give it to them, if they cared to hear it. If they did not— fine."

Here again is this indifference to the audience, to the publication—that is, the broad distribution of one's work and all the distractions this entails—in light of the simple joy of the work.

And though there was always at my fingertips this available joy—it is the writing I enjoy, the actual act of sitting at my desk and looking out my window at the trees, the yard, the sky, and the intermittent sinking into the world of the story at hand, only to rise up and see that sky again, see those trees, see the angle of light through them different now for the sun passing over this all—still I chose, as, I believe, writer's block is an active choice one makes, not to take that joy, instead to natter away my life over this matter of having a book cut from publication for now the second time.

Then, that summer of 1996, a good and dear friend of mine, the poet Jack Myers, helped me remember what I knew all along, despite myself. It was Jack Myers who, as it were, brought me back to that wind and sea. I teach in the low-residency M.F.A. program at Vermont College, where students and faculty spend two weeks together twice a year on the campus, the days filled with workshops and seminars and panel discussions and readings. Jack and I were up in his room in the dorm, and I told him about the book being cut, about the block I was experiencing, about the stagnant quality my life as a writer had taken on.

Writers sometimes talk about stuff like this. Writing and whatnot.

But Jack said something that stuck. He said, "You have to remember why you began to write in the first place: for the fun of it. You have to remember the fun of writing."

The fun of it.

His words reminded me of the obvious fact I had been overlooking, what had fed me this block: publishing had taken precedence over the fun of it.

I wrote my first novel back in 1984 and 1985, started it in September after having graduated with my M.F.A. in May. We had moved from Northampton, Massachusetts, to Columbus, Ohio, during the summer so that I could start up at my first job, teaching remedial English at Ohio State University. The job was a three-year terminal lectureship—it sounds as bad as it was—in which I taught five sections of remedial English per quarter. The writing of the book began for no better reason than that I thought it was time to write a novel, having written nothing longer than twelve pages prior to embarking on the book, my creative thesis a collection of short stories. We had a one-year-old kid then, and lived in a two-bedroom townhome apartment, the two bedrooms upstairs, on the first floor a living room and a kitchen, a basement beneath it all. Each morning I got up between 4:30 and 5:00 and maneuvered my way down the stairs, careful not to step on the third step down, as that board groaned and woke up the baby every time. Then it was to the kitchen for a cup of instant coffee and a piece of toast, all by the light of the stove hood, and then down to the basement and the desk I had stationed there beneath the only window, a narrow thing six feet up that looked out onto the dirt of the flowerbed and through which I could see stars still out when I sat down at that desk. For one year I did this, working on the novel, trying to figure out how to write something this long, writing from 5:00 until 7:00, when my wife got up and the baby, then stopping to make breakfast while Melanie got ready for work, then driving her in, then dropping the baby off at day care, me finally returning about 8:30 or so to the basement, where I would write until 10:30, then head out to Ohio State, and my five classes.

I tell you this all not as some sort of when-I-was-a-kid-I-walked-barefoot-twelve-miles-through-broken-glass-to-get-to-the-typewriter story, but simply to set the stage for the question I had to ask myself every morning once parked at that desk, those stars still out, a story I was writing waiting to be written: who cares?

Who cares, I had to ask, about an RC Cola salesman whose wife had just left him and how he would then live? Who cares about his job, his friends, whether or not he would make it through this piece of his life? Who cares about his life?

And the answer that came to me, while writing a book no one had asked me to write, my family asleep above me, dawn coming up on a day that would involve changing diapers, cooking meals, and ministering to around one hundred freshman who had problems remembering to capitalize the beginning of a sentence, was that I cared. And the truth of this caring was and is and will always be that at the time of invention, in these moments of quiet when the world we see spinning itself out in front of us calls for us to record it, we writers merely amanuenses at the foot of the oracle, the story itself—the truth of this caring is that I will always be the only one in this moment to care.

You are on your own.

It is the care, I submit, that is the fun of writing, that which Jack Myers reminded me of in a cinder-block dorm room. I cared to find out indeed how this RC salesman would make it through, and found in that care the joy of writing. Not that his story was a fun one to tell, not that, like some literary nursemaid, I dictated how he would make it through, not that his making it or not making it would give me joy. None of that. It was simply that caring that made me want to find his story's end.

That care had been lost in me, once the debris of the writing world and all its attendant miseries and triumphs of the ego had superseded why I wanted to write. Again, John Braine's words: "You must remember that you yourself don't matter; only the work matters."

Were all things in my writing life solved with Jack's words? Did I leave Vermont College that summer and magically reenter the world of my novel with newfound gusto and joie de vivre? Of course not. I went home, to where I was still a white male who didn't make good copy for *People* magazine, and tried to write the novel. I wrote still in fits and starts, a particularly big start afforded me by a week that November spent alone in a condo in the mountains of North Carolina, where I managed to get ninety-five pages written and which boosted me toward an end I still couldn't quite see. And by the next spring I had finished the book, finally seen its end, encountered it, written it down.

But of course this triumph, the finishing of a book after two and a half years—the longest it had taken me to write one before this was a little over a year and a half—was only a triumph, as now the book had to go to publishers, find a home. Then began the next part of the story of writing a book: its being submitted for publication. For this is what happens when one finishes a book. Remember Brenda Ueland's words: "Writing was this: an impulse to share with other people a feeling or truth that I myself had." This was my impulse: I write books, and desire them to be read, once the feeling I have had—the story of the novel—has been written down.

My agent then began the dance she describes as professionally taking editors out to lunch. Not a week after she sent the initial salvo out into the hopeful abyss that is the New York publishing world, she called me, said, "I have good news."

She had sold the book, I believed, sold it in only a week, this book over which I had worried so, the one it seemed had had no future for the way I hadn't believed in myself for it. She'd sold it.

But no. It was the memoir she had finally sold. The book I'd put out of mind for the two times it had already been sold and axed. Now it had been sold a third time, and there was a kind of joy in this fact, though perhaps relief might be a better word for it: relief at having placed a book, this with Harcourt Brace, a book about my being white, male, and bad copy for *People*. That book about such normal people.

But then the rejections of the novel began, and again I know you must be thinking everybody should have such problems: he gets a memoir accepted, and complains about a novel. But again: I am a writer. I write books. This is what I do.

And what I had done—had my go at a mystery—began being rejected. One time, two times, four, six, eight times. The rejections came, and came, each with its own rationale for not accepting it. But, on the whole, these rationales seemed permutations of one explanation: Bret Lott is a literary writer, and this is a mystery, and we just don't know how we would market this.

Sure, there were those who thought it too literary, those who thought it too mystery driven, those who figured out whodunit right away and those who thought things too obscure. But most were permutations on the marketing end of things, my agent and I reconnoitering after each one came back, and though this marketability angle seemed to assuage my agent's fears for the book's future—she kept saying there would be an editor brave enough to take it on, to find whatever marketing angle might exist—it didn't do much for me. Writers are, as far as I know, by and large a paranoid lot, and as it was my book being turned down again and again, I began once again to believe it was me, that the book was bad, that it didn't work. And it doesn't take a psychoanalyst to infer from this belief the next step down: I was a bad writer.

See? These fears will never leave you, dear readers. Get used to them now because they will always be with us.

I spent much of that fall not writing, again failing to believe in the gift I have been given.

But wait: there's more: the end of this story has gone on too long already.

When finally the ninth rejection of the book came, my agent and I had a powwow. She called to tell me that she had been thinking about things the night before, and it had come to her for the first time that, perhaps, this book might not get sold, a thought that had crossed and recrossed my mind a million times all autumn long.

Yet something had happened to me around about the eighth rejection, and this is the moment that is key to this entire piece of writing, and which I feel least able to explain in words, the moment I cannot even explain to myself, it is such a mystery to me: around about the eighth rejection, I sat down, in me already this truth that maybe this latest book might not get sold, and started the next book.

It was—is—a novel, the next one. I saw a woman whose husband had died three days before, saw her sitting on their bed, the funeral over, their friends gone home, this woman alone in the house save for her mother-in-law, who had been living with them for the last eight years, since her own husband had died. I saw this.

And I wrote down what I saw in order to begin that journey once again, the one I have no way of knowing how it will turn out, but about which I am compelled to care, because I had seen it.

My agent thought that perhaps this novel that had been turned down nine times might not get sold. But she was calling to suggest, merely as a means of divining whether or not it was indeed the book or the marketability of a literary name like mine that was dictating its being rejected, that we try something new.

"Let's try sending this out under a pen name," she said.

And I said, "Fine," because my eye was on the next, and because I had surrendered the book already. The name, I saw— me—was not important. It was the story—those people in that novel I had spent two and a half years writing—that mattered, that needed to be heard. Not my name, I saw. It was the story.

Two weeks later, the first publisher she sent it to, Villard, an imprint of Random House, bought it, the editor pronouncing it a literary mystery. A week later they found out who I was, and decided straightaway on a marketing strategy: they would publish the book with a nom de plume, and be forthcoming at the same time about who I am. "We'll want you to make appearances," my editor wrote me, "and do publicity probably on a 'literary author tries his hand at something new' theme."

Marketing.

But the punch line to all this, or perhaps the deus ex machina, I haven't yet decided which, is that a month later my editor made the initial presentation to the national sales board for Villard, then called me up to ask if it would be all right to use my real name with the book. The publisher and sales team, she told me, believed in my name, believed it had enough cachet, enough weight and presence to help sell the book.

Go figure.

And now that I have spent all this time telling this story all my own, I see that in fact the best title for this ought to have been "Why Do *I* Write, Anyway?"

I write because I care about the characters I see in my head, care to follow them to their true endings, despite my misgivings about myself, my own ignorance and inabilities, my own vague stabs at trying to limn their paths with the dim light of my imagination. Even in the midst of these falterings—and perhaps in a way because of them—I care, and in this caring find that available joy, writing. And in the surrendering of myself to those characters and by extension to that care, I have found it easier to give up the cares that lead nowhere: the debris of the publishing world and all its attendant miseries and triumphs of the ego.

I have written this down because I am here to write. And once I have written, I want to publish, and this is the way things ought to be: you have a story, and you want it to be heard.

But do not believe that the hearing of it is the end. Do not believe the hearing of it will be the central monument to your life.

Do not believe the hearing of it will bring you a kind of joy that has eluded you all your life. It is certainly its own reward, the hearing of your story, but it is the joy of having written that story—the easing back from the pages in your hand to look up from them to the same old world around you only to see that same old world newly because of those pages in your hand— this is its end, writing.

I write this having published nine books. Easy for me to say that writing is its own end. But I write this also having surrendered my name for the sake of the story, its being heard, and, most importantly, I write this as one having written only the first twenty-five pages of the next, before me the unmapped and ineffable terrain it is up to me and me alone to map.

I am on *my* own.

And like all genuine truths, the only truths worth knowing, this one is immutable, has no context out of which it can be taken, applies to the published and unpublished alike: writing is its own reward, and why I write.

Now, why do you write?

Work

●●●

Toni Cade Bambara once remarked that she was immediately suspicious of characters in stories who didn't have anything to do. "Most of the people I know have a job," she said, and I must admit to the same suspicions: if a character isn't doing something, doesn't have a job, doesn't have a life beyond the mire of his or her own personal life, then I'm not so sure I want to take part.

Grace Paley has said "the slightest story ought to contain the facts of money and blood"; further, in an interview in *Story Quarterly,* she says, "Our family relationships are of the utmost importance, and when they don't exist they're equally important—and how we live, how we make a living. The money in our lives: how we either have it or we don't."

Yet I have found that too often one of the hallmarks of unbelievable writing—that is, we all want to write what will be believed, to write with authority—is that the characters we want to write of, those human beings whose matters of life and death we want to explore, seem more often than not generically employed: someone works at a bank, or in sales, or as a librarian, or as a cashier, or, worse yet, doesn't have anything to do. Too often, I believe, writing that smacks of inauthenticity is writing that is so preoccupied with those matters of the heart that matters of the stomach in our characters' lives, those matters of the wallet, of the car payment and the boss's edicts and the customer bastard always being right, are in fact ignored by us writers.

What we must do, then, to write with authority is to give our characters vocations and avocations outside that mire with which we can so easily become preoccupied, or as a result of or part and parcel to that mire, as jobs in the real world are often responsible for the mire we find ourselves in. Imagine *Moby-Dick* without whaling, *The Grapes of Wrath* without migrant labor, *To the Lighthouse* without Lily Briscoe's painting. Or, more recently, imagine Annie Proulx's *The Shipping News* without *The Shipping News*, Cormac McCarthy's *All the Pretty Horses* without ranching, Marilynne Robinson's *Housekeeping* without the vacant life and hollow home void of any housekeeping whatsoever.

Jobs, then, or the lack thereof, can and do serve the story—sometimes even are the story—rather than simply giving texture or providing a way to have characters blow off time between scenes of interpersonal pathos.

Verisimilitude—that is, the quality of appearing to be true or real—is what we are after in our fiction, but in the same moment we are not solely after this property of believability. Verisimilitude is a necessity, yet the accuracy of our rendering of our characters' lives and their occupations must also speak more largely than simply to the quality of appearing to be true or real;

we must in our writing employ verisimilitude as a means of expanding the story, not as a means to tell the reader what *kind* of person the character is. There are no *kinds* of people; to believe so is to deny the fact we are as human beings individuals; to believe so is to deny the reason for reading: to have revealed to us new worlds, no matter that these worlds may seemingly be as mundane and banal as that of a salesman or lab worker or computer specialist. Rather, the jobs your characters have should be true and real while at the same time letting us know not what these people are, but who these people are, whether they wish to be defined by that job or swear that that job does not define them.

My first novel, *The Man Who Owned Vermont,* is about a man whose wife has left him just before the novel begins; she's left him for reasons dim in his own mind but emotionally acute just the same: he believes himself to be responsible for a miscarriage she had months before at a gas station on the Merritt Parkway on their way down from Northampton, Massachusetts, to visit her parents in New Jersey.

But even this much information, this much plot—a miscarriage, the responsibility, its paralyzing effect on their marriage— came to me not until perhaps fifty or sixty pages into the writing of it. The truth of the book's origin was that one Friday night in September 1984, while watching *Dallas,* I was struck with the truth that if I wanted to get a book published I had to write a novel. I had just graduated from UMass Amherst with my M.F.A. and a collection of stories for my thesis, and figured, judging by the routine return of the book from every publisher I sent it to, that a novel would be easier. Sitting there watching J.R. nearly come to blows with Bobby while that oil portrait of Jock loomed on the wall of the dining room there at Southfork, it came to me that in fact I'd already written the first chapter of a novel, a short story from the collection called "This Plumber," and realized in the next moments that three or four other stories in the collection could, if I fiddled enough with them, be about the same couple, snapshots out of the album of their lives.

"This Plumber" ends with a tentative friendship begun between the narrator, Rick Wheeler, whose wife has left him a couple days before and with a nearly empty apartment, and the plumber, Lonny, who has come to find a leak in his bathroom but doesn't. I remember quite vividly getting up the next morning, Saturday, and sitting down to write a novel, and asking myself, *What happens next?*

What I saw was Rick standing at the window of his apartment watching the plumber walk across the street to his truck, climb in, start the engine. I saw the blue cloud of smoke off his tailpipe, saw him drive away, leaving the narrator to his near-empty apartment and the rest of his life.

What happens next? I asked myself, and it hit me: he has to have a job.

That was when the two-by-four of invention smacked me square in the forehead: let's let him be an RC Cola salesman, I decided, for no good reason other than that I had been an RC Cola salesman for a while in another life, the one before I wanted to be a writer. I say this with all honesty, though fiction writers are by nature a lying bunch: I gave him this job only because I knew about the job and hoped that the experience I had had with the job would make that aspect of his life believable to readers.

So I had him go to work, because it occurred to me that even when your wife leaves you, you still have to show up for work.

For this happenstance, for this serendipitous choice that, in the end, had far greater returns than I could have foreseen, I put forth to you the notion that the jobs your characters ought to have do not have to be invented from whole cloth. They do not, I believe, have to be the jobs of someone else, jobs that carry with them more glamour or more enchantment than jobs you yourself have held; and, by the same token, their jobs don't have to be something beneath your station, as readers can smell condescension a million miles away. I cannot count the number of bad stories about the working class I have read that are bad chiefly because of the jobs chosen for them by the author, who serves more as an omnipotent job placement worker than as a true recorder of the story at hand: inevitably there is in these stories someone who drives an eighteen-wheeler, or who is a short-order cook, or a tired waitress, or a tired cashier at a mini-mart, or a tired wife trying to make ends meet in a tired single-wide trailer. There's always a trailer.

There is, of course, nothing wrong with writing a story about a truck driver who falls in love with a tired waitress who moon-lights at the mini-mart while trying to raise three kids in the single-wide left her by her recently split short-order cook of a husband. The problem is that when you have a character and decide he's the *kind* of person who would make a good truck driver, or who's the *kind* of person who would make a good tired waitress, you are doing the characters a disservice. You are acting as judge rather than court stenographer, when the truth is you've never even had the guts to climb up on the running board of a Peterbilt parked at the truck stop off I-95 to get a good look inside one of those rigs.

Again, using your imagination to write such a story with a character who has such a job is what writing is all about; go ahead and write that story. But understand this: your own job history is the best place to start when it comes to giving your characters occupations.

I said a moment ago that my choice to make Rick Wheeler an RC Cola salesman had far greater returns than I had imagined when I'd seen that was the job he had. What I mean is that once he showed up for work, his life took over, and that job began returning fictive dividends, opportunities for the character to reveal to me whole worlds, characters, settings, all of it stuff I hadn't planned, hadn't thought of, until I let open that door of my own job history.

This was what I saw when I watched him standing out front of a Price Chopper one cold November morning in Northampton, his first day back to work, and what I wrote down:

I got to the front entrance of the place, and stopped. I had my route book, my pens; I had fact sheets on all our sales. I was wearing my light blue RC shirt and navy blue tie, my company-issue navy blue pants, my steel-toed black shoes. I had on my RC jacket. I had everything. I looked up into the blue-black sky, saw a few stars. My breath shot out of me in a cloud as I looked at that cold sky.

My route book under one arm, I turned to the Out door and pulled it open, walked in.

On top of one of the registers was a small radio, the checkstand microphone taped onto the radio's speaker. ZZ Top blasted across the market. Cardboard boxes were everywhere along the front aisle and down each grocery aisle. Stockers, dressed in old jeans and t-shirts, were kneeling, quickly cutting open more boxes, throwing stock onto shelves, facing cans, bottles, what have you.

I breathed in the warm air heavy with bakery smells. I listened to the loud, fast music. I had forgotten over the past few days that Thanksgiving was coming up, was next week. The last time I had been in here was a week ago, and since then they had put up Christmas decorations. Red and green tinsel garlands hung from the fluorescent lights, from the meat case at one end of the store to the bread aisle at the other. Cardboard reindeer hung from the ceiling by fishline. A huge stuffed Santa stood atop the courtesy booth.

I looked around. It felt good to be in here.

This was my entry into Rick Wheeler's life, the life of my character beyond that of the interpersonal pathos that haunted that near-empty apartment, and when suddenly Rick thought, "It felt good to be in here," I was suddenly and irrevocably ushered into the importance of his job to his life now: from then on out, this was his life, and the novel ended up being a chronicle of the ascendancy of his job performance juxtaposed with the spiraling free fall of his personal life, the love for his wife rendered paralyzed by his inability to come to grips with that inner life, the end of love for which he feels responsible.

Here, then, were handed to me all the details of work that I had known dearly and come to hate even more dearly: those fact sheets, and the smell of a grocery store before opening, and how in order to get in before the store is open all you have to do is pull on the Out door, and you're in. And there were those steel-toed shoes, the uniform, the route book, all of it given back to me, though I hated that job, though it was something I have been thankful to have escaped every day I have been alive since the day I gave it up, though I never envisioned there ever being a moment in my writing life when I would face the prospect of tracing the lines of a life that centered precisely, in fact, around RC Cola. That I would spend a piece—a significant chunk—of my life being an RC salesman again.

So this: it was the job I had held that first allowed me to step into the life of this character; then, once inside that grocery store, it was the job I had held that sustained my character through his own personal morass, that mire; and, finally, and perhaps this is the most important point of all, it was the job I had held that allowed my character to purge himself of his own inadvertent anchor, this job driving him toward a kind of faux normalcy while his life—the one that mattered, that of his relationship with his wife—went nearly dead.

Toward the end of the book, Rick must finally face the fact that he still loves his wife. No matter that she has left him, no matter that another love seems in the offing, and no matter as well that his job performance of late has made him next in line for a promotion to sales supervisor, he is faced with the dilemma of going hunting with that plumber from the first chapter or going to work to ride with an executive from headquarters for the sole purpose of grooming him for the promotion. The problem is that on this particular evening he has just been dumped by this new potential love, rebuffed by being forced by her to see that in fact he still loves his wife, so that when Lonny the plumber calls at 3:30 that morning to tell him to get ready to go hunting, he must decide what is most important: his job and riding the route with that executive the next day, going hunting with Lonny, or actually facing his life.

And, as most men are more prone to do than not, he chooses avoiding his life and his job, chooses, of course, to go hunting.

Rick then calls his best friend, the assistant manager of the Price Chopper, Cal—another dividend handed me by letting Rick walk into the store that morning, the assistant manager of the store becoming, unbeknownst or unpreordained by me, Rick's foil throughout the book, a major player I hadn't planned on at all—and asks if Cal wants to go hunting with them. Cal, of course, is still half-asleep as Rick tells him of the plan.

> "Listen," [Cal] said. "Work. What about work?" . . . his voice quiet and cracked.
> "Work," I said. I was standing at the window looking out, and felt the cold outside seeping through the panes of glass. . . .
> "Rick?"
> "Still here," I said. I thought about it, about work. I had to ride with Andros today. Go back to Cal's manager and make that sale cold turkey. Go to my independents, show Andros what I could do. Saturation. Good will. Help stab Mitchell in the back. Help kill him. Hope someone didn't kill me later. I said, "Look. You said yesterday that you didn't care about work. About your market. And I don't care either. I have to get out of here. I have to get out of this place today so I won't go nuts. You come too. You go with us, Lonny and me. He's expecting you." I was quiet, waiting for him to say something, then I said, "I don't care about sales. That's not what I care about. I'll miss a day. I won't die. Neither will you."
> The line was silent a moment, then Cal said, "Let's go."

In this manner the denouement of the novel is begun, and begun only with his shucking of that which made him feel good way back at the beginning, that hiding from his life that the inside of a grocery store and an RC uniform has afforded him, so that, finally, the job that gave his life to me, that sustained his life throughout my writing of the novel, and that he finally jettisons as a means of salvation—basically, the entire engine of the novel, what made it run—was drawn wholly and simply from my own job experience.

The point? Steal mercilessly from your own life, your own jobs, from what you know.

But we only have so much we can steal from ourselves before we have to start looking around, seeking out other jobs for our characters. This leads to my second point about the nature of jobs in fiction, and how to use them: steal from someone else.

Perhaps the best way I can think to do this, however, is if that theft is done stealthily, the more stealthily the better, the best case being that you don't even know you've been stealing that job.

This: look up from your monitor, see what you've been living around, what sorts of occupations have been held by those close to you and revealed to you by what I think of as osmosis, the gradual, often unconscious process of assimilation or absorption.

My second novel, *A Stranger's House,* is told from the point of view of a woman who is a lab technician at a neuroscience and behavior laboratory at UMass. Funny, but my wife worked in the Neuroscience and Behavior laboratory at UMass the whole time we lived there, the three years it took for me to get my M.F.A.

Each short story I finished those three years, once I'd gotten a longhand draft I was pleased with enough to think was approaching being finished, I brought over to the lab, where they had the absolute latest in technology: an IBM Selectric II with a

self-correcting ribbon, so that for three years I sat in the office of
Neuroscience and Behavior typing away at my own fictions
while swirling around me—the professor who ran the lab actually let me sit there and type—were things going on with rabbits, the suturing of nictitating membranes and electric shocks
to particular points in the rabbits' brains that would make those
membranes close, then the subsequent fixing and mounting and
staining of those brains, all in an effort to trace precisely where
in the brain learning occurs in order to produce models of
artificial intelligence.

But at that time, do you think I gave any of that much
thought? No. I wanted to be a writer, dammit, and so I happily
if ignorantly typed away with that magnificent machine at my
masterworks, my stories. This baby had a self-correcting ribbon!

The image that came to me that wanted to begin itself once
I'd finished *The Man Who Owned Vermont*, the picture in my head
that seemed to want the next novel—and this is how the beginning comes, as some image unbidden, something I see happening that intrigues me enough to make me want to follow it out
to whatever end it seems to find of and for itself—was of a
woman standing inside an empty house, her hand at a window,
outside the window, thick woods. "Remote," I heard her say, and
saw behind her a real-estate agent, a woman in a gold sport coat
smiling and nodding.

It was the woman with her hand to the glass I wanted to
know, wanted to listen to, and why she would want to buy
this empty house out in the woods, and what made its being
remote—that word ended up being the first one in the book, her
speaking it to herself but being overheard by the realtor—seem
an important enough reason to buy it.

I started the novel, found in the first chapter that the purchase of the house had more to do with the fact she and her husband could not have children than any sort of real-estate investment. They would buy the house, a fixer-upper, in order, it seemed the two of them knew full well, to rebuild their lives as a means of reconciling themselves to the fact there would be no one after them.

But, I knew by the third chapter when all of this had been settled for me in the first two, that she had to have a job. She couldn't very well sit around her apartment thinking about things, but had to do something. She and her husband were going to buy a house. And so I looked up from my longhand—I didn't yet have a computer, so couldn't very well look up from the monitor—and since I'd already written a book about a guy with the same job I'd held, I couldn't let her be an RC salesman. And so, in an embrace of my own ignorance, I simply looked no further than my wife, and stole from her.

And steal it was, so much so that my editor, once the book was done, made certain that the physical description of the professor running the lab I'd originally written—a description that was, I casually let slip to her one day, pretty much dead on—was changed so that what had been a tall man with a full head of silver hair had been turned into a short guy with male-pattern baldness.

Details I had taken in through the osmosis that had been going on for three years came to me and found their way into the novel, from the coffee machine and mug rack beside the Selectric in the secretary's office—"All our mugs hung on a rack beside the machine. Mine was the one with the rabbits all over it; Sandra's had a nonsensical mathematics equation with no beginning and no end wrapped around it. Wendy's had cartoon drawings of different animals—a turkey, a bear, a rabbit—each saying 'mug.' Paige's was painted to look like a can of RC Cola"—to my wife's constant complaint of how the director of the lab was always leaving his coffee mug on grant proposals, forcing the cover pages to have to be retyped or whited out, resulting in the following fictive version of the truth of my wife's job:

> Inevitably he left coffee rings on important papers, whether reprints or originals, sometimes even grant proposals. Before the laboratory had enough money to hire Paige and Wendy, it had been me who had to take a bottle of Wite-Out and brush over brown spots, even retype pages and letters altogether. I'd bought him a ceramic coaster once, put his coffee on it one morning, but the next day I had come in to find half-a-dozen cigarette butts ground into it, the coffee mug back on a set of proposal guidelines, one more coffee ring to white out.

I knew of the nature of the work they were doing, had even been to the rows of cages in the basement where the rabbits were kept and cared for, had seen, too, a session or two of what was called "running the rabbits," that procedure in which the rabbit was put into a Plexiglas box designed so that only its head protruded, ears and all, the electrodes then placed to wires that had been implanted in the brain, the rabbit then shocked just enough to make it blink, a polygraph beside the whole thing set up recording it all.

But then I hit a wall, some forty pages into the book, when finally that osmosis, the absorption of details that had gone seemingly unnoticed by me those three years and which I was being given back going into the story, tapped out, and I was only, I saw, a guy who'd been typing at my wife's office; those details of the coffee machine and coffee rings would not sustain the depth and breadth of the novel. That is, the point of view of the novel was not from somebody's husband hanging around the office using the typewriter, but from a woman whose job was working here, doing this. Yet the ugly fact was that I didn't know a whole lot about the finer details of the job, knew nothing, too, of the deeper and even darker side of what was done to the rabbits once they had been run, but I knew somehow, in spite of my ignorance and because the material suggested possibilities for meaning and feeling to me—I still wanted to know why she thought this remote house was the one they needed to buy, and now wanted to know how this job and the procedures done to these rabbits she herself cared deeply for spoke more largely to her own inner turmoil, as by this time, too, I'd discovered her father had died when she was young and her mother, an agoraphobic, had died a little less than a year ago—because of all this, I had to do research.

Research. The word itself is repellent to me as a fiction writer, as it suggests all kinds of facts devoid of character, dry recitations and periodic charts and all else. But that legwork is a part of being a writer, just as is sitting at the computer and pensively staring out the window all day long, and so I went back to the laboratory at UMass—by this time we were living in Charleston, South Carolina—and took with me a yellow legal tablet, and pen.

Once there, I asked the director of the lab questions: What was the name of that Plexiglas box they put the rabbits in for "running"? How many rabbits were used in a study? Once through with the running of the rabbits, what was done to them? During the one day I spent there in the lab and listening to him, I received a crash course that gave me more information than I would need to know, as witnessed by the pages of notes I wrote down, pages filled with words and phrases that seemed authoritative in their scientificness: "stereotaxic surgery and atlas," I wrote down, and "perfusion," "Terramycin," "Rongeurs shears." A Gormezano Box was the name of the Plexiglas contraption the rabbits were placed in; it took six rabbits to make a run; and, once through with the running, they were sacrificed.

That was the word that sent me home with all I needed: *sacrificed,* a term it seemed carried with it all kinds of reverberations and ramifications, an oddly gentle and celestial euphemism for the fact those Rongeurs shears were used to pry open the rabbit's skull, its brain having been fixed into a gel hard enough to be extracted from the skull with ease to then be frozen and sliced and stained and mounted. All to better understand the brain, to come closer to seeing into how the mind worked.

Which, it finally came clear to me late in the book, was precisely what the protagonist, Claire, puzzles over throughout her life, in light of parents who are gone and a body that has betrayed her in its inability to give her the next life and yet still insists each month on menstruating: *who am I,* this term *sacrifice* speaks to Claire, *and why am I here?*

That word and its euphemistic nature, then, became the cornerstone of one of the climactic scenes, an integral one in that she finally recognizes her job as being some twisted kind of reflection on the truth of her own life, its emptiness wrapped in the cloak of seeming necessity:

Sacrifice was the word used, uttered by Will and Sandra and myself and in all the literature, a word that veiled what we did, hid the fact that we killed them next; a word that elevated things somewhat, and made us feel, perhaps, that indeed we were doing some sort of favor to these animals for whom we'd already destroyed some center of thinking, cells that made them blink in anticipation.

Sacrifice.

Still I was listening to my father, the image of my dream still with me four days later, seared into my own brain every time I went to the bathroom, each time I had to pull out the swelled and brown-red tampon and drop it between my legs into the toilet, where I would flush the thing down, those bits of possible life shed voluntarily by my own body, a traitor. Still I bled, and bled, and bled, as though this steady flush from my own system were one long reiteration of the truth: I could not have a child, my pregnant body only a dream. Nothing more. Some accident of God, who'd given me this. An accident.

Sacrifice.

After this final sacrifice, she walks away from her job, throws herself fully and dangerously into the renovations on the house they have bought, only to find that here, too, she cannot escape herself, as she has imagined she might by trying to leave the lab.

It is this associative power between self and vocation, the verisimilitude of the job coupled with its attendant window into the hearts of our characters, that is the heart of fiction itself. If I had not made that initial step into her job at the lab through nothing but the accumulation of details I had no part in accumulating, only that I was present at that Selectric, and if it had

not been for that depletion of details that led to my doing research, this novel would not have worked, the revelations of the
interior country of her own heart left unmapped. Yet once that
research had been accomplished, the most important thing I
could do as the writer of her story was to record her own ex-
trapolation from it, her own abandonment of self in order to
find herself.

Trust, then, in what intrigues you in your entry into these
worlds others inhabit; trust in the jobs others near you may have
held in order to give yourself that entry into those lives. But
once that initial intrigue disappears, once that theft bottoms out
or pulls up short, do the necessary homework, and then aban-
don it. Let the jobs, again, speak for themselves to the characters
you see making a living, trying to be who they are.

And, finally, once you've stolen vocations from yourself and
those you love, then *invent from whole cloth*. Make it up. Fake it.
Lie through your teeth.

Which is what I did with *Reed's Beach*, my fourth novel, about
a computer specialist who works at the Hess building in Woodbridge, New Jersey, and his wife, and one twenty-four-hour period in February.

What do I know about computers? For one thing, I own a
Mac precisely because, as my friends who own PCs lament, all
you do with a Mac is point at a picture and click on it to make
things happen. That's exactly the point, I tell them.

This novel began not as an image of something happening,
but at the discovery of a real place, Reed's Beach, a strip of summer cottages on the Delaware side of Cape May my in-laws and
my wife and I happened to drive through one afternoon in 1982.
It was a haunting place, accessed only by a thin gravel road out

across tidal marsh, two rows of arrogantly shabby homes at the end of it, those on the shore side built on pylons so that, I had imagined that day, you might hear the tide moving in and out while you slept at night.

That was it, the single impression I was given that long ago. I was still a grad student—you may have figured out by now how fruitful my years were as a grad student—and hadn't yet published a single story, hadn't yet finished my thesis, hadn't yet watched that episode of *Dallas*. It wasn't until nine years later, when after finishing my third novel, *Jewel*, I returned in my imagination and memory to that setting, its haunting still sharp in me, to begin the novel that would be set there, its plot premise precipitated by a short story I had written, a story only 250 words long and which appeared in my collection *A Dream of Old Leaves* in 1989. That story would fit the setting that had been with me all these years, I realized. In it, a father wakes up in the middle of the night, hears his child breathing in the next room, walks in the dark to the child's room, turns on the light, and sees the room, empty, the bed made up sloppily, kid stuff out on the desk. The child has died, one realizes, and the father takes in what he hopes is a dream, but realizes is not.

That settled—the story of how a couple either accommodates their lives to this loss or doesn't, combined with a haunting landscape—I knew my character needed a job, one that would somehow allow him and his wife access to this cottage on the ocean. And again, as always, I thought about what I know, thought about New Jersey, about what jobs there might be that would get them into this place.

Ed Bly. That's what I came up with. Ed Bly, a friend of ours from all the way back when my wife was in high school in Matawan, New Jersey. Ed and Gail Bly were our best friends in

Jersey, and he worked as a computer specialist for payroll at Hess, and I knew then that the character in my novel worked at Hess and would be granted a kind of asylum at the summer cottage by one of the executives there, one of the men who could afford such a place.

There. First three chapters.

But now there was this pesky job I had to get the character, Hugh Walker, back to—this was February, and they could use the cottage, loaned to them by an executive vice president, Mr. Halford, as long as they want, so long as Hugh is in to work in Woodbridge at least three days a week—and there was this matter of making it all believable. And so we went up to Jersey and visited Ed and Gail, and I asked him a few numskull questions both out of laziness and the notion that I wanted to wing it, to try and see for myself if I couldn't hack my way through this job and have the trail behind me bear some semblance of believability.

This time I was only after terms, words, pure lingo—*batch*, he gave me, a term meaning a group of programs, and *ABEND*, or the abnormal ending of a program due to an error inside it. He gave me *MSA trade rep*, the person at MSA, the company who made the payroll software used at Hess, who could troubleshoot a problem, and the term *SOC7*, which I cannot to this day explain or understand in any way other than to say this is a very bad thing and will wreck a program. He even gave me a bad joke they passed among themselves at Hess: What's a SOC4? To cover your feet.

Thus armed, I went into the novel knowing that Hugh and his wife, Laura, are in Mr. Halford's summer cottage in February, sent there by Mr. Halford in order to straighten out the emotional vertigo left to him and his wife after the death of their son. But Hugh, once back to work, gets tied up with a SOC7 that prevents payroll checks for the state of Rhode Island from being printed out, and that threatens to keep him from ever heading back to the cottage.

For Hugh has resolved to fix this problem, just as he has vowed to keep in him thoughts of his son and his accidental death always, their child having died a little over three months before. Laura seems to him totally incapable of mourning their son's death, contributing to his being stymied at exactly how one can go on living after this grief has been visited upon oneself.

Now it was tap-dance time. Throughout the novel Hugh is addressing the SOC7 while well-meaning officemates, including Ed Blankenship, his immediate supervisor, and Mr. Halford, stop in to inquire as to how he is doing. Of course Hugh doesn't want to let show his ever-present wound, though he's nursing it always, and so dismisses their inquiries or assigns them as being inquiries into the problem at hand: this SOC7.

Until, once everyone has left the building and he is left alone with the problem, and the two preoccupations—one tragic, the other business—unite, become one and the same endeavor:

> Now he was alone, and there were no spectators. Only the mission of completing the batch, getting Rhode Island to stop sweating.
>
> He'd looked at the screen, at the mass of equations and quotient derivations, the language that spoke only in 1s and 0s, a world so simple and logical and devoid of all grief that he wanted to sink into it, be swallowed by so many *Yes* and *No* and *No* and *Yes* qualifiers.
>
> He stared at the screen and suddenly glimpsed the

world he wanted to inhabit, the one in which only those *Yes* and *No* questions could be asked, and he saw for an instant the giant arc of loss and love, the two of them intertwined across the expanse of time—he had only the rest of his life to live, only that—these arcs stretching all the way back to one single, quiet question: *Do you love your son?*

The floor was silent save for the high-pitched hiss, barely audible, of the screen before him, the computer itself.

Yes, he typed in.

He looked at the word there, saw how incongruous it was against the mass of numbers and letters, punctuation marks and slashes and spaces. This was the real world, he thought, the one in which he actually existed: random numbers, random letters, inexplicable symbols.

He deleted the word *Yes,* but placed inside himself the knowledge the answer still existed. He hadn't typed over the word, hadn't put in no. He'd only deleted, and it had seemed, too, this parallel to the exact truth of accident— his child had been deleted, not negated, not denied—was some sort of dark miracle. His son no longer existed, but did. He'd lived, breathed, spoken. This was fact.

And then he saw the SOC7, the data exception.

Like all exceptions, it lay in plain sight, easy once one had found the source:

{I/771:R91}I¬}

It was there just four lines below where he had typed in the word *Yes;* he would not have seen it, he believed, were he not here to hear only the hiss of electricity through circuits.

He deleted the line, given the access code by the MSA trade rep earlier that afternoon, when they'd chosen to return his call from that morning. Then he entered the correct equation:

$$\{I/771:R91I\neg\}$$

It had been only a misplaced end bracket, right there after the second numeral 1, a bracket placed too early in the derivation, but one that shut off the line before it was completed.

A typo.

An accident.

He pushed himself away from the screen, heard the wheels of the chair across the hard plastic carpet guard beneath him. He stared at the screen, his hands in his lap.

Only an accident, an end bracket placed too soon, cutting off the equation to let the whole of the program ground to its own ABEND, every equation after the one cut short therefore nonsense, worthless.

He closed his eyes.

An accident.

What do I know of computers? Nothing, really. Only that those words, that jargon, combined with the haunted landscape that had been with me for years and the tiny story of a father's walk down a dark hallway in the middle of the night, afforded me entrance into a story that mattered finally and most importantly to me. Hugh does not leave his job in indifference, as does Rick in *The Man Who Owned Vermont;* he doesn't leave in terror and disgust, as does Claire in *A Stranger's House.* Instead, his job has delivered him to a place where he can see perhaps the same thing these other characters have: that his job is in many ways himself, a diviner and definer of character, for better and worse.

Of course the stuff we want to write about in the novel and in the short story involves matters of the heart, matters of life and death, matters of consequence and weight and measure. Matters that we all as writers and, more importantly, as human beings believe are worthy of our attentions and ruminations precisely because we are human beings.

Yet we are also here for the duration, have lives that exist beyond our lives as writers, though there are plenty of times when I wish I could simply sit there at my desk and look pensively out my window all day long and have nothing more to do than that, and get away with calling it writing.

But the mortgage beckons—wails, actually. And there is the car payment, and the insurance, too, and of course the gas. Tuition payments are coming due, and the dentist, and the vet. Not to mention the groceries, and clothes, and all else, right on down to the Biggie Fries and Frostie from Wendy's on the way home, taking from your pocket the last two dollars and eleven cents you have on you. There are at any given moment any number of larger and smaller millstones round my neck and yours both, these millstones weighing us down, dragging at us in the way the worries of the world drag at us all.

We have to work for a living.

And the truth is that our lives as workers, as bank tellers or salespeople or librarians or cashiers, are all too often the most real part of us, the most graphic and powerful and demanding and debilitating and triumphant, though the grind of it may seem unworthy of even the smallest attentions from us. We want to *write,* dammit, to be *writers.* Who cares about my life as a soda pop salesman or lab tech or computer specialist, when I'm addressing these matters worthy of our attentions and ruminations, these matters of life and death?

I submit that if in our fiction we are not representing the working lives of our characters as fully and vividly and graphically as these facts of our own lives are vivid and graphic and full, then we will not, as Conrad said of his hope for his fiction, "render the highest possible justice to the visible universe."

We will not tell the truth.

For this reason, then, take the jobs your characters have seriously, investing in them the same level of disaster and joy we find in the jobs we all of us must hold down day in and day out. Find in these jobs the associations with matters of the heart we all want to write about. And once there—at that juncture of work and love, whether arrived at through occupations you know intimately or don't have a clue about—let your characters find themselves, for better and worse. And, it is to be hoped, it is in this manner that we can find ourselves, no matter—or perhaps in celebration of—that mortgage wailing, that car payment, the food we have to buy so that we might eat it, and live.

Handling Time

●●

For me, one of the most interesting aspects of my favorite books is the way time is handled, the manner in which the author lets spin out of his or her hand the tale before us through its idiosyncratic sense of *chronos*.

One of the best examples is the novel *First Light*, by Charles Baxter, in which time moves backward. From the epigraph of the book—"Life can only be understood backwards, but it must be lived forwards," from Kierkegaard—we already see what is in store, the architecture available, already in motion before the story even begins. Another favorite is *Machine Dreams*, by Jayne Anne Phillips, a novel that tells the story of a West Virginia family between World War II and Vietnam; the element of time is here handled through Phillips's choices of point of view, encompassing everything from letters to first-person reminiscences to third-person narratives to dreams. The result is a bridge over time that is remarkably intricate in its design, yet seamless in the same moment.

And this bridging of vast spans of time isn't relegated only to novels: "Mid-Air," by Frank Conroy, captures in only a few pages the entire life of a man whose psychology and, therefore, his brief tenure here on earth have both been informed by the opening episode of the story, in which his apparently insane father, after being chased by men in white, dangles the boy by his belt from high atop a building. The rest of the story is given over to brief snapshots, present-tense episodes in which the character, growing older, encounters puzzling and anxiety-filled situations that, unbeknownst to him but clear to the reader, involve echoes of that first incident.

And there is the incredibly beautiful, indeed perfect story "Bullet in the Brain," by Tobias Wolff, who, in the course of a couple of pages, lets flash before our eyes not just what a man in the fraction of an instant before death remembers, but what he does not: we know his entire life.

The reason I'm forever intrigued by the way authors handle time in their novels and stories, however, isn't merely artistic altruism; that is, it's not just because I love these works of fiction. I'd be lying if I didn't admit to the other element, the selfish reason I as an author look at these stories with envy.

Because it seems in my own writing life I've never gotten it right, or at least have never gotten time handled in the way I want when I first start out.

Dana Gioia writes in his wonderful poem "The Next Poem" about the way things seem before we get our hands on them: "How much better it seems now / Than when it is finally written." We all have desires for our work, see in it before we attempt it the way we believe the piece ought to be wrought. And it is that gap between how we see the work move before us and the fact of its moving in and of itself that has always been the central paradox of writing: the work we create must breathe on its own.

Easier said than done, this idea of letting the story go, and allowing it to tell itself in its own sweet time.

Case in point:

Remember that Friday night in September 1984, when I was watching *Dallas*? There in front of the TV I'd realized that in fact I'd already written the first chapter of a novel, but there also came to me the first visual beyond this realization that I had a few components already in hand.

The image, then, that drove me to sit down and start that first novel was of an RC salesman standing in the back room of a grocery store the day after Christmas, bagboys tossing unsold Christmas trees into the huge baling machine back there. In fact, the first extant piece of that novel is the scrawled line "Day after Christmas—bagboys baling Christmas trees," written on the back of an orientation letter from the remedial English department, the only piece of paper close at hand when the image came to me, J.R. and Bobby still tussling on the floor. That was the image I wanted in that novel, this feeling of remorse, of things already terminated and out of our hands: Christmas over, trees baled.

It was that scene I wanted, the story to last, in my mind's eye, at least a month, from the November morning "This Plumber" takes place on through to that sad and remote ending, the day after Christmas.

The problem, though, was that I'd never written anything longer than twelve pages prior to embarking on the book. When

I went downstairs each morning to try and find out how much I cared about Rick the RC salesman, there sat before me an interminable amount of time to write about—a month!—when every story I'd written thus far lasted, perhaps, fifteen, twenty minutes out of a life.

What did I do? How could I get to that day after Christmas? How could I make time pass?

First, and most importantly, I just began writing. This is by no means a glib answer, a jolly pitch to dismiss a genuine concern. Rather, it is the truth of what it means to be a writer: John Gardner writes in *On Becoming a Novelist* (no creative writing student of mine ever emerges from one of my courses without having read and reread this book), "It's the sheer act of writing, more than anything else, that makes a writer." Common sense, numskull logic. But you'd be surprised at the amount of handwringing that goes on by people who want to write, but are too fearful to begin.

And I had a plan: in my mind, I had before me those three other stories, placed them in my line of sight as though they were stepping stones across a stream. On the other side, the opposite shore, lay that final scene, the day after Christmas.

So that each writing day had a kind of goal: I wrote the next line, asking, *What happens next, and what associations might that action bring to the character's mind?* with the next story my endpoint; I wanted merely to get to the next stone in the stream, that next story I'd already written.

But the novel, though happily participating in this scheme, had other ideas about where it wanted to go and when, though I kept that scrawled line on my desk every day, looked at it, focused on it as a means to drive me forward through time and, though I continued to write to that next stone, the story.

Yet, during the next year it took me to write the book, the novel wrestled itself free from what I intended. Time took on its own standard, and the story and its associations only lasted from the week before Thanksgiving to the sixth of December. That opposite shore, finally, existed only in my plans, however well meaning and heartfelt.

Next case:

My third novel, *Jewel*, I knew would start in 1943 and end somewhere around 1984. Again I couldn't for the life of me figure how to do it, cover time for all those years; the longest amount of time I'd ever covered was in the novel just prior to *Jewel*, *A Stranger's House*, which spanned only four months.

Yet here stood forty-one years before me, waiting to be recorded, made believable. Made real, when in fact if one were to engage in actually recording the fact of a life lived, attempting to make reality real, forty-one years would last more pages than I could have written in forty-one years. And still, looking at the beginning of my third novel—would I ever get the hang of this?—the question mocked me: how do you just get time to go by?

So, armed only with my ignorance and a desire to tell the story of a woman who has six children, five of whom are born in a log cabin in the Mississippi wilderness, the sixth a Down syndrome baby born in a country hospital, I started writing.

And found, around page 54 or so, I hadn't yet let one day pass. I'd started before sunup this March day in 1943, and hadn't yet let go. They were only now sitting down to supper. I still had forty-one years to go, minus a day.

But, lucky for me, the light of ingenuity and inspiration also dawned on me around page 54, when I realized that I could make as many years pass by as I wished, if I could only illuminate a single day out of the year I chose to skip to next. That is, this one day in 1943 could stand for her life here, now; the next section of the book, whichever year it turned out to be, would chronicle another single day; if I could simply tell the truth of that day, reveal what happens and the associations the details of that day bring to Jewel's mind, then I wouldn't have to worry about precisely how to get time to go by. Time would handle itself.

Thus I settled on a plan: this section, 1943, would be named "Monday," the next section "Tuesday," and so on, until, finally, I would reach 1984, the year I wanted to end Jewel's story with, and call it, simply, "Sunday," the day of rest. It seemed fitting, logical, even poetic: she would be eighty years old then, her children, all six of them, including the Down syndrome baby she had had to raise, would be grown, and she would be alone. Beautiful, I figured.

I finished the Monday section, that day ending after dark, the night going cold, in Jewel the knowledge she was going to have a sixth child. The section, finally, weighed in at around ninety manuscript pages.

Then I started on "Tuesday." When I finished that section, and before, truly, I even noticed it, five months had gone by in that single section, from October and the birth of the baby through to February of the next year, ending with Jewel's decision not to give up the baby to an institution.

So much for the light of ingenuity and inspiration.

But I think the most important thing anyone—especially me—can learn from these examples is the way time and its attendant structural possibilities, though seemingly apparent, right there before us and ready to be followed, oftentimes erupts of its own, gives its life to itself, the writer be damned. And that's good. Faulkner, when asked once by an interviewer if he didn't feel obliged somehow to help out characters in his stories who'd gotten themselves into trouble, replied, "I don't have time. By that time I'm running along behind them with a pencil trying to put down what they say and do."

Time, therefore, and its handling are always in flux in my writing life, much to my consternation, even if things eventually work out on their own, the story revealed to me only after the fact. That's how I work, the *chronos* of a book providing for itself during production and, I hope, seeming inevitable by the time the work is done.

What has worked for me, of course, is letting time go, that framework surrendered.

Ah. Surrender.

This is the rub, finally, to becoming a writer of any merit: the surrendering of one's will to the work at hand. And yet if that surrender does not occur—if the writer does not acknowledge in holding the reins of the story the story's sovereignty—then all the writer will ever have on his hands will be an ordered mess of words imposed by an outside entity, the writer himself. It is when the writer imposes the order he sees on the story, imposes his own *chronos* and not the organic timekeeping of the story itself, that the story will surrender its own will to live, and will die in a kind of logos-suicide.

So how to keep this from happening?

Listen, I believe, above all else. In John Fowles's "Notes on an Unfinished Novel," he recounts an instance of trying to make his character do his own bidding, and finding himself "stuck this morning to find a good answer from Sarah at the climax of a scene. . . . After an hour over this one wretched sentence, I realized that she had in fact been telling me what to do: silence from her was better than any line she might have said."

The same goes for how to let the time of the novel find itself: listen to what I can only think of as the heartbeat of your character's story, the rhythm of associations combined with the action you see before you, both evolving in and of themselves to form what is the time of the story. Not your time.

I believe, too, that the problem of handling time is intrinsic to the associative powers of the story at hand. That is, the associations that are made with whatever situations, circumstances, characters—whatever—that are encroaching upon your character's waking moments will carry with them elements of time and its passage.

I recently read a novel manuscript by one of my graduate students, and found, though the story took place over six months, and though there were plenty of interesting landscapes, a whole host of bright and lively characters, comic scenes throughout, even a murder and some bumbling though well-meaning detectives thrown in, that by the time I got to the end of the work, I was exhausted, felt as though I had watched five or six months go by in just a matter of hours. I felt as though I hadn't been able to breathe, felt nearly suffocated, though the story did not have in its execution any signals that this was the feeling the story intended its readers to feel.

This was because the story had been allowed no associations; it was purely surface, occurring only in the here and now, and the crushing suffocation of the work had to do with the fact the narrator, a sixteen-year-old kid, simply hadn't been allowed a moment's reflection on what was taking place around him, hadn't been allowed to let track back through his mind what these people and places meant to him, when the story as given—that present surface—and the character as given—a boy a bit bewildered by the way certain members of his family have betrayed him—demanded that breathing room, that acknowledgment that our hands on the reins are indeed merely gestures as to who's in control.

Were my novels, as a result of relinquishing my plans for their time frames—one headed toward an initial image I saw before ever beginning the book, the other mapped out like a battle plan of the days of the week—weakened because of the surrender? There is no way to tell, no forecasting whether or not one finished book is better than one never written, though those plans seemed so shiny, so available and certain.

But I do know that the books were written, achieved lives of their own.

Certainly it pays to have a plan, a ballpark idea of what might occur. But by allowing associations to be made—whether in the form of flashbacks, or impressions, dreams, influences, even shapes in the clouds or the way shadows change between late August and the first day of September—time will reel itself in the direction it so chooses, so long as the author is listening to the story, allowing its heartbeat to become the author's own.

Listen. Plan, and be willing to give up that plan. Let the story and its characters associate freely with their available world, and find in this freedom a *chronos* that works well and only with this story, the one spinning out of your hand in its own genuine sweet time.

Toward a Definition of Creative Nonfiction

The Reverend Francis Kilvert, an English curate in the Welsh border region, kept a journal of his life—where he went, what he did, what he dreamt, who he knew, and what he thought—from 1870 to 1879. In the journal he wrote, "Why do I keep this voluminous journal? I can hardly tell. Partly because life appears to me such a curious and wonderful thing that it almost seems a pity that even such a humble and uneventful life as mine should pass altogether away without some record such as this." Although I doubt anyone here has read the journal, *Kilvert's Diary*, published in 1941 and reprinted in 1960, and though no one here's life has been altered by said journal, the book serves as a beautiful and moving and genuine glimpse into country life of that time nonetheless. All well and good, I know you must be thinking, but how does it help define what creative nonfiction is?

That passage serves, I hold, to illuminate as best as any passage from any piece of literature I can find the longing we each of us carry, or ought to carry, in our hearts as human beings first, and as writers second. Creative nonfiction is, in one form and another, for better and worse, in triumph and failure, the attempt to keep from passing altogether away the lives we have lived.

And though that may sound like a definitive pronouncement on what creative nonfiction is, I mean what I say in giving this essay the title it has: Toward a Definition of Creative Nonfiction. We aren't going to arrive anywhere here. We can no more understand what creative nonfiction is by trying to define it than we can learn how to ride a bike by looking at a bicycle tire, a set of handlebars, the bicycle chain itself. Sure, we'll have something of an idea, maybe a glimpse into the importance of finding your balance when we look at how narrow those tires are. But until we get on that thing and try to steer it with this weirdly twisted metal tube and actually try to synchronize pushing down on the pedals and pushing forward at the same time, we won't have a clue.

Any definition of true worth to you as a writer will and must come to you experientially. What creative nonfiction is will reveal itself to you only at the back end of things, once you have written it. Kilvert wrote his journal in the midst of his life, looking back at what had happened that day, trying to piece together the meaning of his life from the shards of it, however exquisitely beautiful or sharply painful they were. But it was the piecing together of it that mattered, and that matters to us here, today.

As I said earlier, we as human beings are pattern makers, a species desirous of order, no matter how much we as "artists" may masquerade otherwise. Yet looking back at our lives to find that order—and here is the sticky part—must always be not an effort to reorder our lives as we want them to be seen; rather, we are after, in creative nonfiction, an understanding of what it is that has happened, and in that way to see order, however chaotic it may be.

For it is in creative nonfiction we try to divine, from what we have done, who we have known, what we have dreamt, and how we have failed, an order to this universe: ourselves. "The test of a first-rate intelligence," F. Scott Fitzgerald wrote in his landmark essay "The Crack-Up," "is the ability to hold two opposed ideas in the mind at the same time, and still retain the ability to function." The two opposed ideas of creative nonfiction are finding order in chaos without reforming chaos into order; retaining the ability to function is the act of writing all this down for someone else to understand.

So let's begin with just that much: a desire not to let slip altogether away our lives as we have known them, and to put an order—again, for better and worse—to our days.

Please note here at the beginning that creative nonfiction can take any form, from the letter to the list, from the biography to the memoir, from the journal to the obituary. When I say we are trying to find order in what has happened, I by no means mean creative nonfiction is simply writing about what happened to me. Rather, it is writing about oneself in relation to the subject at hand. A book review is creative nonfiction in that it is a written record of the reviewer in relation to the book in question; John Krakauer's fantastic book *Into the Wild* is a biography of an idealistic young man, Chris McCandless, who upon graduation from college disappeared into the wild, his decomposed body found four months later in an abandoned bus in the

Alaskan wilderness, yet the biography becomes creative non-fiction as the author increasingly identifies himself with the young man, increasingly recognizing in the stupidity of the boy's folly his own reckless self—Krakauer sees himself in relation to the subject at hand: the death of Chris McCandless. This essay itself is a form of creative nonfiction in that it is my attempt at defining an abstract through the smallest of apertures: my own experience in relation to creative nonfiction. So creative nonfiction is not solely, *What happened to me today, and why is it important?*

I think it safe, however, to say that the term *creative nonfiction* can be and often is a euphemism for the personal essay, and my earlier assertion that creative nonfiction is understood only through its being written is borne out rather handily in the meaning of the word *essay* itself.

The French word *essai* means the attempt, the trial run, the test. Michel de Montaigne, considered the writer who identified if not invented the form as a form, was the first to use the word *essai* to describe his writings, the first collection of which was entitled strangely enough *Essais,* and which was written from 1572 to 1574. This notion of the attempt, of testing one's words lined up in an order one deems close enough to reveal a personal understanding so that all may have that same understanding is, and will always be, only an attempt. The essay as trial run is inherent to any definition of creative nonfiction; you will only come to know this form by running your own tests.

Montaigne, a landowner and lawyer from a nominally wealthy family in the Périgord region of France, wrote out of his own interests, but wrote convinced that it was his own interest as a human being in a matter or topic at hand that made his at-

tempts universal: "Each man bears the entire form of man's estate," he wrote, and therefore, he reasoned, what he was attempting to render in words might make his attempts of interest
to all. Phillip Lopate, in his indispensable anthology *The Art of
the Personal Essay*, writes, "What Montaigne tells us about himself is peculiarly, charmingly specific and daily: he is on the
short side, has a loud, abrasive voice, suffers from painful kidney
stones, scratches his ears a lot (the insides itch), loves sauces, is
not sure radishes agree with him, does his best thinking on
horseback, prefers glass to metal cups, moves his bowels regu-
larly in the morning, and so on. It is as if the self were a new
continent, and Montaigne its first explorer."

The self as continent, and you its first explorer: another
definition of creative nonfiction. For self, however at the center
of what you are writing or however tangential, must inform the
heart of the tale you are telling. It is indeed self that is the creative element of creative nonfiction. Without you and who you
are, a piece of writing that tells what happened is simply
nonfiction: a police report. But when I begin to incorporate the
sad and glorious fact that the way I see it shapes and forms what
is to be seen, I end up with creative nonfiction.

As a kind of sidebar, I'd like to interject here the fact that one
doesn't have to have had a bizarre life before that life becomes
worthy of writing about. Contrary to popular belief, that belief
borne out by even the most cursory look at the lineup of victim-
authors on afternoon and morning TV talk shows and evening
newsmagazines, one's life needn't have been wracked by incest
or murder or poorly executed plastic surgery to be worthy of examination. Which is, of course, not to say that those lives are not
worth writing about. They most certainly are. But E. B. White's

words from the introduction to his *Letters of E. B. White* speak as eloquently as I have seen to this matter of whether or not one's life has been miserable enough to record:

> If an unhappy childhood is indispensable for a writer, I am ill-equipped: I missed out on all that and was neither deprived nor unloved. It would be inaccurate, however, to say that my childhood was untroubled. The normal fears and worries of every child were in me developed to a high degree; every day was an awesome prospect. I was uneasy about practically everything: the uncertainty of the future, the dark of the attic, the panoply and discipline of school, the transitoriness of life, the mystery of the church and of God, the frailty of the body, the sadness of afternoon, the shadow of sex, the distant challenge of love and marriage, the far-off problem of a livelihood. I brooded about them all, lived with them day by day. Being the youngest in a large family, I was usually in a crowd but often felt lonely and removed. I took to writing early, to assuage my uneasiness and collect my thoughts, and I was a busy writer long before I went into long pants.

These normal fears, if we have been paying the least bit of attention to our lives, inform us all; and if E. B. White, the greatest American essayist of the last century, found in that uneasiness the material for a lifetime, we too have all we need.

But how do we look at ourselves in order best to inform our readers that who we are matters, and that we are worthy of their attention? In the Tyndale Commentary on the Book of Proverbs, Derek Kidner writes that the sayings and aphorisms of King Solomon, and to a lesser degree Lemuel and Agur, constitute "not a portrait album of a book of manners: [the Book of Proverbs] offers a key to life. The samples of behavior which it holds up to view are all assessed by one criterion, which could be summed up in the question, 'Is this wisdom, or is this folly?' " I believe that this same criterion is one that helps define creative nonfiction as well. In examining the self as continent, in seeing the way self shades and informs the meaning of what has happened, the writer must be inquiring of himself, *Is this wisdom, or is this folly?* The self as inquisitor of self is integral to an examination of one's life; it calls for a kind of ruthlessness about seeing oneself in relation to others: Why did I do that? What was I thinking? Who was I trying to kid? What did I hope to achieve? These questions must be asked, and asked with all the candor and courage and objectivity one can muster, though objectivity is an abstract to be hoped for, and not to be achieved; it is, after all, you who is writing about you.

Which brings me to another major point on our way toward a definition: creative nonfiction cannot at any time be self-serving. There is no room here for grandstanding of oneself. To my way of thinking—and this is me speaking as a follower of Christ, and therefore one well aware of my transgressions, my iniquities, my falling short of the glory of God—ninety-nine times out of a hundred the answer to the question *Is this wisdom, or is this folly?* is, Folly. Hands down.

Phillip Lopate writes, "The enemy of the personal essay is self-righteousness, not just because it is tiresome and ugly in itself, but because it slows down the dialectic of self-questioning. . . . The essayist is someone who lives with the guilty knowledge that he is 'prejudiced' (Mencken called his essay collections *Prejudices*) and has a strong predisposition for or against certain everyday phenomena. It then becomes his business to attend to these inner signals, these stomach growls, these seemingly indefensible intuitions, and try to analyze what lies underneath them, the better to judge them."

So, our definition thus far: a desire not to let slip altogether away our lives as we have known them; to put an order, for better and worse, to our days; this is only a test; the self as continent, you its first explorer; is this wisdom, or is this folly?; no self-righteousness.

This last point, however, seems at odds with the entire notion of the personal essay, all this business about me: isn't talk about myself in relation to others by definition egotistical? Wasn't I taught in seventh grade never to include *I* in an essay? Who cares about what I think in the first place?

Thoreau, in answer to this assertion we have had pounded into our heads most of our lives, wrote in the opening of *Walden,* "In most books the I, or first person, is omitted; in this it will be retained; that, in respect to egotism, is the main difference. We commonly do not remember that it is, after all, always the first person that is speaking." And if one is honestly seeking to understand, circling unself-righteously one's relation to events, places, people—whatever the subject of the essay—then that search's chances of being construed as egotistical will be dismissed. Seventeenth-century English writer Alexander Smith wrote, "The speaking about oneself is not necessarily offensive. A modest, truthful man speaks better about himself than about anything else, and on that subject his speech is likely to be most profitable to his hearers. . . . If he be without taint of boastfulness, of self-sufficiency, of hungry vanity, the world will not press the charge home."

Another element of any definition of creative nonfiction must include the form's circling bent, its way of looking again and again at itself from all angles in order to see itself most fully; the result is literary triangulation, a finding of the subject in a three-dimensional grid through digression, full-frontal assault, guerrilla tactics, and humble servitude, all in an effort, simply, to see. The creative nonfiction form attempts in whatever way it can to grab hold hard and sure its subject in any manner possible. Eudora Welty writes in *One Writer's Beginnings,* "In writing, as in life, the connections of all sorts of relationships and kinds lie in wait of discovery, and give out their signals to the Geiger counter of the charged imagination, once it is drawn into the right field. . . . What I do make my stories out of is the whole fund of my feelings, my responses to the real experiences of my own life, to the relationships that formed and changed it, that I have given most of myself to, and so learned my way toward a dramatic counterpart." The dramatic counterpart of which she here writes is, of course, her stories—fiction—but I maintain that this "whole fund" of feelings, the complete range of our responses to our own real experiences, must inform creative nonfiction as well. Only when we use our "whole fund" can we circle our subjects in the most complete way, wringing from our stores of knowledge and wisdom and the attendant recognition of how little we have of both—the essence of who we are—then coupling those recognitions with what in fact we do not know altogether, will we find what we have come looking for: ourselves and, by grace and by luck, the larger world perhaps we hadn't seen before.

Lopate writes, "The personal essay is the reverse of that set of Chinese boxes that you keep opening, only to find a smaller one within. Here you start with the small—the package of flaws and limits—and suddenly find a slightly larger container, insinuated by the essay's successful articulation and the writer's self-knowledge."

I agree with Lopate in how the essay reveals larger and larger selves in itself, but rather than the Chinese box, the image that comes to my mind is that of the Russian nesting dolls, one person inside another inside another. But instead of finding smaller selves inside the self, the opposite occurs, as with Lopate's boxes: we find nested inside that smallest of selves a larger self, and a larger inside that, until we come to the whole of humanity within our own hearts.

Now back to our definition: a desire not to let slip altogether away our life as we have known it; to put an order, for better and worse, to our days; this is only a test; the self as continent, you its first explorer; is this wisdom, or is this folly?; no self-righteousness, though it is always the first person talking; circle the subject to see it most whole.

I'm saving perhaps the most conundrum-like element for nearly last.

What role, we have to ask once all these prior elements are taken into account, does truth have here?

If you look at the pieces of our definition thus far, each one contains within it the angle of perception: the fact that it is only me who is seeing. That is, I don't want to let slip away my life as I have seen it, but who is to say I am telling the truth? In my attempt to put order to my days, am I deluding myself, inflicting an order that was and is now nowhere to be seen? If this is only a test, who is to say I pass? If I am the explorer of my self as continent, what does my discovery matter—didn't Leif Eriksson set up shop in North America five hundred years before Columbus discovered the place? Isn't one man's wisdom another man's folly? How do I know if I'm not being self-righteous unless there's somebody outside myself to cut me down to size? In circling my subject, isn't it me who determines my course, my longitude and latitude, and therefore am I, by definition, being the most subjective of anyone on planet Earth when it comes to my subject?

The answer to each and every one of these questions is: *continue to question*. Only through rigorous and ruthless questioning of the self can we hope to arrive at any kind of truth.

If you wish to understand creative nonfiction, hope to find a definition, then it is up to you to embrace the fact that, as Montaigne saw, "Each man bears the entire form of man's estate." Inherent to that form are the eccentricities, egotism, foolishness, and fraud of all mankind; inherent as well are the wisdom and self-recognition, the worth and value and merit available to mankind, once enough scouring of what we know and do not know has taken place. V. S. Pritchett, in his memoir *Midnight Oil*, wrote, "The true autobiography of this egotist is exposed in all its intimate foliage in his work. But there is a period when a writer has not yet become one, or, just having become one, is struggling to form his talent, and it is from this period that I have selected most of the scenes and people in this book. It is a selection, and it is neither a confession nor a volume of literary reminiscences, but as far as I am able I have put in my 'truth.'"

Pritchett puts the word *truth* in quotation marks; he predicates it with the possessive pronoun *my*. We must recognize that this is the deepest truth we can hope to attain on our own: quotation marks, calling it our own. Only when we have scoured as clean as possible by self-inquiry, even interrogation, what we perceive can we approach calling it truth; and even then that crutch of the quotation marks and the assignation of who it belongs to—me—must be acknowledged.

Finally, on this long-winded trek toward a definition of the undefinable, we have to try to further illuminate why we write creative nonfiction. Certainly that first element—a desire not to let slip altogether away our lives as we have known them—is a beginning point, but simply trying to capture our lives before they slip away seems more reactive than proactive. Writing is, I believe, both, and so any definition must encompass both the reactive and the proactive.

Karen Blixen, a.k.a. Isak Dinesen, in a dinner meeting speech she gave in 1959 at the National Institute of Arts and Letters in New York, addressed the subject "On Mottoes of My Life." In the speech she said, "The family of Finch-Hatton, of England, have on their crest the device *Je responderay,* 'I will answer.' . . . I liked it so much I asked Denys . . . if I might have it for my own. He generously made me a present of it and even had a seal cut for me, with the words carved on it. The device was meaningful and dear to me for many reasons, two in particular. The first . . . was its high evaluation of the idea of the answer in itself. For an answer is a rarer thing than is generally imagined. There are many highly intelligent people who have no answer at all in them. . . . Secondly, I liked the Finch-Hatton device for its ethical content. I will answer for what I say or do; I will answer to the impression I make. I will be responsible."

This is the proactive element of creative nonfiction, and the final element of my *essai* to define creative writing: our responsibility as human beings to answer for and to our lives. It is a responsibility that must encompass all the elements laid out in all this talk about definitions; it is a responsibility that must be woven through the recognition of the fleeting nature of this span of days we have been given, woven through our attempt to see order in chaos, through our understanding that we are only attempting this test, and through our being the first explorers of the continent of ourselves. This responsibility to answer for and to ourselves must be woven through the interrogation of self as to whether this is folly or wisdom, through the pledge to humility and to avoiding the abyss of self-righteousness, through the recognition that it is always and only me—the first person—talking, and through the relentless circling of the subject to see it most completely. And this responsibility to answer for and to ourselves must be woven through our recognition that the only truth I can hope to approach will finally and always and only be my truth.

But if we are rigorous enough, fearless enough, and humble enough to attempt this responsibility, this way of seeing—for creative nonfiction, like fiction, like poetry, is simply and complexly a way of seeing—the rewards we will reap will be great: we will understand. To understand, and nothing more, and that is everything.

Against Technique

● ●

As the title I've inflicted upon the following suggests, I have some definite feelings about the whole notion of *technique* in writing, but now that I'm sitting down to write this, the truth is that I can tell you just about anything.

I could write here, for instance, about Boy Scout Troop 20, over at Mt. Pleasant Presbyterian—I was an assistant scoutmaster— and how when we went backpacking in the Pisgah National Forest a few years ago, I was afraid both my sons—Zeb, then age fourteen, and Jacob, twelve—though avid campers, might find it awfully difficult to hike the seven miles up to the top of Shining Rock. They hadn't actually backpacked before, and the trail climbed thirty-five hundred feet in elevation over those seven miles, ending at the mountaintop and six thousand feet. Of course, as their father, I was afraid they'd get whipped, tired out, start whining, and even gave them a stern lecture before we headed up the trail about the need for patience, for stamina, for not being whiners when the trail got tough.

I could tell you of how I was stunned, however, when, nearing the top of the mountain, me dead last, bringing up the rear and feeling as though I were about to die, I looked up the trail and saw Zeb taking the backpack off one of the younger kids who had all but given up, the boy sobbing on the trailside because of how heavy his pack was and how tired he was and how we would never get to the campsite. I watched my son put that younger boy's backpack over his own shoulder, then look back down the trail at me, and ask, "Dad, you all right?"

I nodded, out of breath, unable to say a word, and watched him turn, head on up the mountain, two backpacks on now, one on each shoulder. He'd already pitched his tent by the time I made it to camp.

And during these few pages I could tell you about my other son, Jacob, who stunned me on this same campout as well, the two of us sharing a tent at the top of this mountain on a night that got down to eleven degrees. I'd spent myself that day, so exhausted by the time I climbed into the tent with Jake that I didn't even want to refill my canteen from the spring someone'd found up there. I'd drunk all my water on the way up, and when in the middle of the night I wanted more water, and knew I had none, I asked Jake if he had any.

He said he did, and got out his canteen. In the bottom of it was only a dribble, enough to wet a parched mouth. But this was my son's water I was about to drain, and so I asked him if he wanted it.

"No," he said. "You take it. I can wait till morning."

And I drank it.

And I could tell you, too, of how every time I get up in the middle of the night for a drink of water now, I think of Jacob as I stand in the darkness at the sink, the cup to my lips, and that night in a tent, the wind on a mountaintop tracing through the trees above us while I drank the last of my son's water, and I think of Zeb, too, and his taking that kid's backpack and checking on me, and I am thankful and puzzled at once: given a father like me, one who'd underestimated his kids, who'd figured they'd end up whining and whipped; given me, how is it they turned out like that?

But if I were to tell you about all this as my way of filling my self-allotted pages here, you might get the idea I wasn't paying attention to the occasion at hand: an essay on techniques. You might think I was a little nuts even, if I were to go on any more about my boys, and I haven't even started in about my wife, Melanie, whom I love and still can't figure out after twenty-four years of marriage, that inability to figure her out one of the great things about her I love. If I started on her, then you might even begin to look at your watches, wonder when the heck this guy will be through.

But there's a reason I'm not talking about what you may think I ought to be talking about: writing. And it's this: I know nothing.

It's true. My holding court on technique makes me apprehensive because, after having written six novels, two story collections, and a memoir—geez, after having been on *Oprah*!—I believe now more than ever what Socrates said quite awhile ago: the greatest level of wisdom man can hope to attain is the realization of how little he knows.

Not only is this notion Socratic, it is also biblical: Proverbs 13:10 says, "Through presumption comes nothing but strife, but with those who receive counsel is wisdom." And this notion is, too, literary: Steinbeck, while he was writing *The Grapes of Wrath*—he did it in one hundred days—kept a daily journal, and on the eighteenth day wrote, "If only I could do this book properly it would be one of the really fine books and a truly American book. But I am assailed with my own ignorance and inability. I'll just have to work from a background of these."

So I'm not the first one to know nothing.

This not knowing, too, has always pervaded my writing life. *Fathers, Sons, and Brothers* began not as a memoir—that decision was made by my agent when, after the book had been turned down several times, she decided to change the title page from *Fathers, Sons, and Brothers: Personal Essays* to *Fathers, Sons, and Brothers: A Memoir*, the next publisher to see it then buying it— nor did it begin even as a group of personal essays. The term creative nonfiction was something I'd never heard of—I don't even know if it existed—when the writing of the book began, way back in 1984, me an instructor of remedial English at Ohio State University, loaded with those five sections a quarter.

That first quarter, the head of the department—Ohio State had an entire department of Remedial English, twenty-six instructors in all—mandated that we write an essay for the next departmental meeting so that we could feel firsthand what we were expecting of our students, and so be better teachers.

An essay? I'd been writing them all through high school, college, and grad school—the M.F.A. from UMass then was made up of the same number of academic hours as the Ph.D., and so we M.F.A. people took the same classes as the Ph.D.s, and wrote and were evaluated by the same standards. I'd written essays before. And my identification with my students didn't need to be any deeper: I'd been writing every day by then for four years, had just finished my M.F.A. thesis, was launched upon a novel. Empathy for my students? Come on.

But it was an assignment, and I had to do it.

And it just so happened that my firstborn, by then a little over one and speaking quite well, upon waking would call out "Mommy!" first thing, no matter that Melanie and I had worked out an even-steven system of tending to him each day, one day me the first to go in there, change his diaper, get him going, the next day Melanie.

But that didn't matter to Zeb—the same guy who picked up that smaller sobbing scout's backpack and carried it up a mountain, but only after he'd checked on me—because every morning Zeb cried out "Mommy!" whether it was me or Melanie to answer him.

A fact that, at the time, bothered me: I was Mommy in the mornings, though he'd eventually get around to calling me Daddy sometime later in the day. But the first one through his door, the first one to respond each morning, was Mommy, whether I liked it or not.

So I wrote an essay about this strange fact of identity, of parenthood, of duty and obligation no matter the name you were given.

And promptly put it away, once it had been turned in and assessed by the head of the department as "cute." But its writing had taught me something: there were things—factual things—going on in my own life that deserved my attention as a writer, things that, once the scrim of fiction had been raised to reveal I was left with the fact of people I knew and loved, I might want to write about.

Because the essay about my son calling me Mommy gave me, in the writing of it, a discovery about the truth of who I am as a parent: it didn't matter what he called me. He needed me, and loved me, and I him. This was a point I had not thought of when I began writing it, began it as only an assignment, this odd moment out of my life worth looking at a little more closely, yielding, unbidden by me, this discovery.

Thus began the memoir, though it would be nine years before it would be anywhere near a book, as over those nine years I simply sat down now and again and wrote the fact of what was happening with my children, and my perceptions of that fact, and found in what I saw associations to the often numskull things they were doing with the always numskull things I and my own brothers did as we were growing up, and associations as well with stories I had heard of the profoundly numskull things my father and his brothers did to one another growing up. And here were essays, true stories, all of them put in a drawer because the discoveries each yielded, about who I was and who my siblings and children and father all were, was reward enough for the writing.

They were stories I was writing, I came to realize. Stories, but with this element woven through them: they had happened.

Then one day, I pulled an essay from the drawer, one written about a year before and simply collecting that proverbial dust. I read it, liked it, shrugged, and decided to send it to a journal, *Antioch Review*, because I had read in a recent issue one of the essays there, about what I cannot now recall. But it seemed worthy of consideration.

And Robert Fogarty took it. And then I started sending other essays out, and writing more, the idea now, finally, taking shape back in the brain that perhaps this could be a book.

Nothing I knew would ever happen—nothing I even considered—when first I sat down to write that assignment.

I know nothing.

So deep is my sense of ignorance, in fact, that I make certain to do my best to pass this character trait on to my writing students, both fiction and creative nonfiction, making them repeat after me each class session my motto: I know nothing. I really make them say that.

What knowing nothing means, finally, is that one must strip himself of all notions of what he believes he knows about the world and the way it works. The majority of my students come into class with a sense of wanting to set the world straight—the world being, generally speaking, a euphemism for Mom and/or Dad. Consequently I get tons of message-laden essays and stories about how awful and bourgeois and fake everything is, the kind of stories Chekhov raged on about being the realm of the propagandist and preacher.

But once one gives up these notions of knowing a thing or two—all his prejudices about the world—one is left with a new world, which is, of course, and paradoxically, the same old one.

Yet now it's new terrain, undiscovered, left to this new explorer, the one who knows nothing and who now, armed with this ignorance, stupidity, and tendency to stare, sees things newly, and becomes, again if he is lucky, "one on whom nothing is lost," to quote Henry James's old line.

What this explorer will ultimately discover is his own heart, who he is in the midst of all the know-it-alls of the world. Because this is what I am after in all this knowing of nothing: finding out who, in fact, I am.

Even now I can't attribute this notion to myself, this finding of self through surrender of self, but must admit to plagiarism, as it was Christ who gave us this supreme of paradoxes: "For whoever wishes to save his life will lose it; but whoever loses his life for My sake and the gospel's shall save it. For what does it profit a man to gain the whole world, and forfeit his soul?"

Which is why it scares me to be here before you like some sort of possessor of the mystery to what it means to be a writer. It means having children who have been in Boy Scouts, and it means a wife I can't figure out. And it means, too, the books I have written, though they come way down the list. They are only crude maps of the worlds I've done my best to walk through, rough charts of the seas I've done my best to navigate. And still I know nothing.

Steinbeck, by the way, on the ninety-ninth day of the one hundred he took to write *The Grapes of Wrath,* noted in his journal, "I don't know. I only hope it is some good. I have very grave doubts sometimes. I don't want this to seem hurried. It must be just as slow and measured as the rest but I am sure of one thing—it isn't the great book I had hoped it would be. It's just a run-of-the-mill book. And the awful thing is that it is absolutely the best I can do."

Then this, the most telling line of all: "Now to work on it."

I don't say I know nothing to be glib, or funny. Truly. It's simply to say, I'm not sure how to write. I'm just not sure.

It seems to be all about scene. And all about detail. It's all about one good sentence placed after another and another until, when you look up at the end of the day, you see through the pale light of late afternoon that you have pieced together a story— whether fact or fiction—that might, if you are lucky, be larger than itself. That might, if you are beyond lucky and in fact blessed, be larger than *you.*

And the path toward the discovery of a world larger than the self is arrived at through the simple act and art of paying attention, as Flannery O'Connor exhorts us in that quote about staring, about that "grain of stupidity that the writer of fiction can hardly do without."

Here is something else Flannery O'Connor had to say, this about the making of art, and an additional testimony to why I feel apprehensive about talking about what I know as a means to teach you something about writing:

> St. Thomas called art "reason making." This is a very cold and very beautiful definition, and if it is unpopular today, this is because reason has lost ground among us. As grace and nature have been separated, so imagination and reason have been separated, and this always means an end to art. The artist uses his reason to discover an answering reason in everything he sees. For him, to be reasonable is to find, in the object, in the situation, in the sequence, the spirit which makes it itself. This is not an easy or simple thing to do. It is to intrude upon the timeless, and that is only done by the violence of a single-minded respect for the truth.
>
> It follows from all this that there is no technique that can be discovered and applied to make it possible for one to write. If you go to a school where there are classes in writing, these classes should not be to teach you how to write, but to teach you the limits and possibilities of words and the respect due them. One thing that is always with the writer—no matter how long he has written or how good he is—is the continuing process of learning how to write. As soon as the writer "learns to write," as soon as he knows what he is going to find, and discovers a way to say what he knew all along, or worse still, a way to say nothing, he is finished. If a writer is any good, what he makes will have its source in a realm much larger than that which

his conscious mind can encompass and will always be a greater surprise to him than it can ever be to his reader.

The writer's discovery is integral, is the lifeblood, is the art itself—not what it is to be discovered. It is the discovery taking place in the heart of the author that is the experience of art.

And what can bring about that experience of discovery can only be the solitude of the writer's life; the life, that is, away from people like me telling you how to write. Franz Kafka wrote, in *Letters to Felice*, about the main ingredient to a successful life as a writer:

> Writing means revealing oneself to excess; that utmost of self-revelation and surrender, in which a human being, when involved with others, would feel he was losing himself, and from which, therefore, he will always shrink as long as he is in his right mind. . . . Even that degree of self-revelation and surrender is not enough for writing. Writing that springs from the surface of existence—when there is no other way and the deeper wells have dried up—is nothing, and collapses the moment a truer emotion makes that surface shake. This is why one can never be alone enough when one writes, why there can never be enough silence around when one writes, why even night is not night enough. This is why there is never enough time at one's disposal, for the roads are long and it is easy to go astray.

It is solitude the writer needs in order to discover that which he alone can and must discover. Yet there exists a possible danger that the utter solitude required for writing and writing well may create: there is the possibility that a kind of myopia might set in, a sense of distorted vision that may result in looking too closely at the work at hand. Of thinking too much.

Here is Arthur Stanley Eddington, a scientist and writer from the earlier part of the last century, writing in *The Nature of the Physical World*. Please note here that I think it perfectly acceptable to slug in "a writer who thinks too much" for the term "scientific man" in the following passage:

> I am standing on the threshold about to enter a room. It is a complicated business. In the first place I must shove against an atmosphere pressing with a force of fourteen pounds on every square inch of my body. I must make sure of landing on a plank traveling at twenty miles a second round the sun—a fraction of a second too early or too late, the plank would be miles away. I must do this while hanging from a round planet head outward into space, and with a wind of aether blowing at no one knows how many miles a second through every interstice of my body. The plank has no solidity of substance. To step on it is like stepping on a swarm of flies. Shall I not slip through? No, if I make the venture one of the flies hits me and gives a boost up again; I fall again and am knocked upwards by another fly; and so on. I may hope that the net result will be that I remain about steady; but if unfortunately I should slip through the floor or be boosted too violently up to the ceiling, the occurrence would be, not a violation of the laws of Nature, but a rare coincidence. . . .
>
> Verily, it is easier for a camel to pass through the eye of a needle than for a scientific man [or a writer who thinks too much] to pass through a door. And whether the door be barn door or church door it might be wiser that he should consent to be an ordinary man and walk in rather

than wait till all the difficulties involved in a really scientific ingress [or, in our case, an artistic technique] are resolved.

Thinking too much about how to disallows movement, disallows life, and so disallows art. Witness this dinner exchange with Chekhov, from the memoirs of Lydia Avilova:

At the table we sat side by side.

"She does a bit of writing too," Sergei Nikolyevich informed Chekhov indulgently. "And there's something there . . . A spark . . . And an idea . . . Even if it's very slight, there's thought in every story."

Chekhov turned to me and smiled.

"Leave out thoughts!" he said. "I beg you, please. What's the use? One has to write what one sees, what one feels, truthfully, sincerely. I am often asked what it was that I was wanting to say in this or that story. To these questions I never have any answer. There is nothing I want to say. My concern is to write, not to teach! And I can write about anything you like," he added with a smile. "Tell me to write about this bottle, and I will give you a story entitled The Bottle. Living, truthful images generate thought, but thought cannot create an image."

And this, from Henry James, describing "an English novelist, a woman of genius," as regards the perception that a writer needs to know and know authoritatively before he or she can embark upon the hidden road of a work of art:

She was much commended for the impression she had managed to give in one of her tales, of the nature and way of life of the French Protestant youth. She had been asked where she learned so much about this recondite being, she had been congratulated on her peculiar opportunities. These opportunities consisted in her having once, in Paris, as she ascended a staircase, passed an open door where, in the household of a pasteur, some of the young Protestants were seated at table round a finished meal. The glimpse made a picture, it lasted only a moment, but that moment was experience.

This is the wellspring of writing, whether fiction or creative nonfiction: the simple act and art of paying attention.

It is the wellspring, I believe, because it is paying attention that can then become, in the strange and unpredictable alchemy of the mind, experience; experience is then sifted through the heart into perception; perception is then burnished by the soul into understanding; and understanding, through the colossal and unfathomable compression of the writer's solitude and tenacity and fearless faith in the intuitive, then yields finally, like diamonds from coal, the inescapable truth of you.

Because it is only through paying attention by you, the author, that art will be made. It is and always will be only you seeing, if I may paraphrase a bit brazenly Thoreau's unintended dictum, "It is, after all, always the first person that is speaking." This seemingly claustrophobic fact is in truth—whether in the art of the essay or of fiction, and why can't we also include poetry as well?—the single most liberating force behind the making of art.

Henry James writes in his preface to *The Portrait of a Lady* of this apparently stultifying actuality—that there is only one portal into art—and of the human being's false expectation, because we are as human beings believers, whether we like it or not, in patterns and categories and order, that there ought to be a kind of generic unity to ways of seeing, and hence a way that can be taught to all.

The house of fiction [James writes] has in short not one window, but a million—a number of possible windows not to be reckoned; rather, every one of which has been pierced, or is still pierceable, in its vast front, by the need of the individual vision and by the pressure of the individual will. These apertures, of dissimilar shape and size, hang so, all together, over the human scene that we might have expected of them a greater sameness of report than we find. They are but windows at the best, mere holes in a dead wall, disconnected, perched aloft; they are not hinged doors opening straight upon life. But they have this mark of their own that at each of them stands a figure with a pair of eyes, or at least with a field-glass, which forms, again and again, for observation, a unique instrument, insuring to the person making use of it an impression distinct from every other. He and his neighbours are watching the same show, but one seeing more where the other sees less, one seeing black where the other sees white, one seeing big where the other sees small, one seeing coarse where the other sees fine. And so on, and so on; there is fortunately no saying on what, for the particular pair of eyes, the window may not open; "fortunately" by reason, precisely, of this incalculability of range. The spreading field, the human scene, is the "choice of subject"; the pierced aperture, either broad or balconied or slit-like and low-browed, is the "literary form"; they are, singly or together, as nothing without the posted presence of the watcher—without, in other words, the consciousness of the artist.

And though he is here writing of fiction, it has been my own discovery as a writer of both fiction and creative nonfiction that the same holds true for both. Without the consciousness of the artist—without the unique being seeing the human condition we all of us see each and every day of our lives through the singular window behind which we stand—there can be no art, whether of the fictive form or factual, and the unfortunate and blessed truth of this is that there can be no teaching to you any technique for being the unique being you are. To believe in technique is to pretend there is only a certain size and shape window that will allow us to see, and to pretend there is only one watcher behind them all. To pretend there is a technique or even a compendium of techniques that will give you you, is to pretend there is only one essay, and one story, and one poem.

Technique, of course, can be taught. Its result, however, is a kind of uniformity that yields not art, but artifice. I know this firsthand, having twice been on the Literature Fellowships panel for the National Endowment for the Arts in both fiction and creative nonfiction. After reading hundreds and hundreds of manuscripts, the one constant I saw that arose from them all, the one common denominator—and it was, let me assure you, a most common denominator—was the technical competence of the works at hand. They were technically competent. Nothing more, nothing less. Only competence—creative nonfiction and fiction alike all told well, whether in any number of obtuse or conventional ways—that revealed a kind of routine verbal acumen, but which had, sad to say, no heart. No soul. Only windows all alike and all in a row, behind them merely automatons dressed in various costumes of style, but automatons nonetheless.

Because when the consciousness of the artist is neglected for technique, the result is often serviceable, may resemble truth, but it will never be alive. This is from Arthur Schopenhauer, the nineteenth-century German philosopher and supreme pessimist, on the folly of making reality more important than its perception by the artist:

> Waxwork figures make no aesthetic impression and are consequently not works of art (in the aesthetic sense), although when they are well made they produce a far greater illusion of reality than the best picture or statue can and if imitation of the actual were the aim of art would have to be accorded the first rank. For they seem to present not the pure form but with it the material as well, so that they bring about the illusion that the thing itself is standing there. The true work of art leads us from that which exists only once and never again, i.e., the individual, to that which exists perpetually and time and time again in innumerable manifestations . . . but the waxwork figure appears to present the individual itself, that is to say that which exists only once and never again, but without that which lends value to such fleeting existence, without life. That is why the waxwork evokes a feeling of horror; it produces the effect of a rigid corpse.

And yet.

And yet, I must acknowledge that the selection of those moments from reality, those shards of the real life we lead, must be assembled into the living, breathing thing we call art. It is the solitary "posted presence" who must piece together the disparate, the chaotic, the once concrete and now only memory, into being.

Which, of course, leads us to our desire for technique. As I said, because we are pattern makers, we want to believe, we want to hope, that the selection process—choosing from the whole of what we see through the totally idiosyncratic aperture of who we are—is a kind of one-size-fits-all process. But it isn't.

Again, Henry James, this time from the preface to *The Spoils of Poynton,* on the nature of selection:

Life being all inclusion and confusion, and art being all discrimination and selection, the latter, in search of the hard latent value with which alone it is concerned, sniffs round the mass as instinctively and unerringly as a dog suspicious of some buried bone. . . . Beyond the first step of the actual case, the case that constitutes for [the artist] his germ, his vital particle, his grain of gold, life persistently blunders and deviates, loses herself in the sand. The reason is of course that life has no direct sense whatever for the subject and is capable, luckily for us, of nothing but splendid waste. . . . If life, presenting us the germ, and left merely to herself in such a business, gives the case away, almost always, before we can stop her, what are the signs for our guidance, what the primary laws for a saving selection . . . ? The answer may be after all that mysteries here elude us, that general considerations fail or mislead, and that even the fondest of artists need ask no wider range than the logic of the particular case. The particular case, or in other words his relation to a given subject, once the relation is established, forms in itself a little world of exercise and agitation. Let him hold himself perhaps supremely fortunate if he can meet half the questions with which that air alone may swarm.

We may be blessed, James says, if we can wrestle half the questions that rise up about us. Yet questions still persist: how do you do it?

What is the *technique*?

The technique, alas, is that there is no technique, save for the one you yourself will hammer out.

Here is Annie Dillard, on the nature of the impossible and necessary moment when the writer finds himself between the proverbial rock and a hard place—and you and I will find ourselves, if we want to write, and if we are blessed enough to persevere, precisely there many times over:

> Writing every book, the writer must solve two problems: Can it be done? and, Can I do it? Every book has an intrinsic impossibility, which its writer discovers as soon as his first excitement dwindles. The problem is structural; it is insoluble; it is why no one can ever write this book. Complex stories, essays, and poems have this problem, too—the prohibitive structural defect the writer wishes he had never noticed. [Now, if I may say this without seeming condescending, please pay attention:] He writes it in spite of that. He finds ways to minimize the difficulty; he strengthens other virtues; he cantilevers the whole narrative out into thin air, and it holds. And if it can be done, then he can do it, and only he. For there is nothing in the material for this book that suggests to anyone but him alone its possibilities for meaning and feeling.

The possibilities for meaning and feeling will be, please note, only suggested to you by the being looking through the aperture before you at the human scene before us all. *By* you, *through* you, *to* you.

And the one element that is indispensable to realizing the meaning and feeling of the art you make will have to be—can only be—the unquenchably burning, unappeasably hungry, naggingly doubtful, and exhaustively self-motivated desire to find meaning in the way you see. It is only "by the pressure of the individual will" that the window before you will be pierced; that piercing of the aperture through your will and yours only is, finally, the only technique you will ever need. "If it can be done," to repeat Annie Dillard, "then he can do it, and only he."

It is the meaning and feeling *you* own that will give you the means to say what it is you mean and feel.

And it is this single-minded doing, finally, that is the true triumph of art, the true liberation only the artist can enjoy: the discovery you can. Here is accomplishment, and here is reward, no matter how piecemeal the final product, no matter how intimately one will know its flaws, no matter how rough the road was to get here. "Stories and novels . . . are makeshift things," writes Richard Ford in this essay "Reading." "They originate in strong, disorderly impulses; are supplied by random accumulations of life-in-words; and proceed in their creation by mischance, faulty memory, distorted understanding, weariness, deceit of almost every imaginable kind, by luck and by the stresses of increasingly inadequate vocabulary and wandering imagination—with the result often being a straining, barely containable object held in fierce and sometimes insufficient control. And there is nothing wrong with that."

Nothing wrong at all. But only in the discovery of an autonomous and benevolent republic of art created through your own rigorous intellectual, emotional, spiritual, and even physical effort—it takes a lot of individual will to make yourself sit on your butt day in and day out to write a book—will you ever, ever, finally, finally, know how this all happens.

Here will be your technique.

Ursula K. Le Guin writes, in *Very Far Away from Anywhere Else*, of precisely this moment of understanding technique, however ex post facto it may arrive: "Everything had to be right. You didn't know for sure what was going to happen when you finally did get it all right: you had to get it right to find out. . . . If [you] did it absolutely right, it might turn out to be true. To be the truth."

We want technique, I believe, because we fear the future. We have been to the future, operate here every day, and we know it to be messy. Unpredictable. Frightening, because it is out of our control. Technique, we figure, will help us in our predictions of the future. Knowing techniques will help us make what hasn't yet been made easier to make. It will make the future neat for us, and predictable, and in our control, and so that future will, through the glory of technique, be less frightening, and so less intimidating.

But it is the inherent frightening and intimidating nature of the creation of art that makes the discovery the reward of art, and the reward to the artist. The predictable future is the future the true artist can live without. It is precisely the unforeseeable moment of discovery that in fact fuels the desire of the true artist, and hence fuels true art.

The truth will be arrived at only through arriving at it. This will only be how you will know technique.

And perhaps the only true way I can come near to educating you is simply to let you know that I am eternally looking through my own window, straining my own individual will to see. In spite of the books I have written—and I mean that truly, in spite of, as each book written gives me the foolish belief I know how to write, when damned if the next one up provides its own set of insoluble problems it will always be left up to me and me alone to solve—in spite of all those books, I too am continually duct-taping together my own disorderly impulses and faulty memory; I too am trying to find the limits and possibilities of words and trying to accord them the respect they are due.

I am only trying to walk into the room.

I don't say this as a cop-out, by the way. I don't say I am trying to figure this out as a means to shirk the responsibilities of my role as perhaps a seasoned guide toward the limits of words and the respect due them. Rather, I tell this all to you in the hope that we will together not find ourselves at the end of our educations as writers—that is, at the end of our lives—as knowledgeable but empty; as technically competent and artistically soulless.

Here is George Eliot, writing in *Middlemarch:* "It is an uneasy lot at best," she writes, "to be what we call highly taught and yet not to enjoy: to be present at this great spectacle of life and never be liberated from a small hungry shivering self—never to be fully possessed by the glory we behold, never to have our consciousness rapturously transformed into the vividness of a thought, the ardour of a passion, the energy of an action, but always to be scholarly and uninspired, ambitious and timid, scrupulous and dimsighted."

The end of this story is that my boys did precisely what I said they did at the outset of this all: Zeb carried that second backpack, Jacob gave me that water. And I did, the fool that I am, what I said I did as well: I gave my kids a stern lecture; I stumbled exhausted into camp, the last man up; I drained my younger son's last drop of water.

Then we hiked another day, and another, and we went home, climbed into our warm beds, and slept.

But in the middle of that night, me sore, bleary with exhaustion, I woke up, thirsty, and went for a glass of water, and had no choice but to think of my son giving me water, and had no choice as well but to see my older son carrying two backpacks up the mountain, him turning first to check on me.

And it is only now I see the gift they have both given me. Not the look at me, Zeb's checking on me, and not Jake's last dribble of water. The true gift, the one I am only now realizing as I write this down right here, right now, for the purposes of this essay on technique, is the memory I have of them giving that gift, the picture in my head of a momentary beneficence that will last as long as I have memory. And the gift back to them from me, however small, is my writing this discovery down for you, right now.

I only hope this all has been enough, because I have nothing else to tell you about the nature of technique. Only this reiteration: it's all about scene; it's all about detail; it's all about one good sentence placed after another and another.

And, finally, there is this exhortation: go, and do not think. Disavow uninspired scholarship, timid ambition, scrupulous dimsightedness on your way to the discovery that awaits in the making of art. Let ignorance, inability, and stupidity be the flag of the day. Pay attention recklessly. Strain to see through the window of your own artistic consciousness in the exhilarating and frightening and liberating knowledge that there is no path to the waterfall, and there are a million paths to the waterfall, and there is, too, only one path. Yours.

A Home, a House: On Writing and Rejection

I've kept close to me for more than twenty years now my copy of John Gardner's *On Becoming a Novelist*. I've kept it close not only for the fact it was a gift to me from my literary hero, Raymond Carver, out of his own personal stash of author's copies (he wrote the foreword) way back when I was still a grad student working on my M.F.A. and trying to figure out how to write. That seems reason enough to have kept it close.

But I keep it close for an even more important reason: it's a book that has spoken to me more clearly than any book I have ever read on what it means to be a writer. Yet I must confess that there is a chapter in the book that I have fairly ignored for quite some time. It's the next-to-last chapter, titled "Publication and Survival." Here's the first paragraph:

> Some writing teachers claim that the student writer should never think about publishing but should simply

work hard at learning his craft—presumably on the assumption that if the student learns his craft well enough, publication will take care of itself. The assumption is probably right, but I'm suspicious of those who argue it: I suspect the teacher's main motive is the wish not to be bugged by students about publication. And in any case, though it's generally true that one ought not to publish until one has work worth publishing, and that when one does have such work, publication is not likely to prove inordinately difficult, it is nevertheless a fact of life that young writers do want to get published, and to tell them "Hush and eat your spinach" is to evade real problems.

I was brought back to this chapter by a couple of recent bits of news from former students of mine at the Vermont College M.F.A. program. It seems these two students have received rejections of their respective novels—and they are worried. Even fretful. I told them both that their novels were good, and publishable, back when they got the old heave-ho from the program. That is, once they graduated. I told them both that they should pursue publication. But it has not yet happened, and they are worried, though there are between them only eight to ten rejections combined.

So, this essay. Because I don't want anyone to be fretful when facing the cold hard truth about the pursuit of publication. And I don't want to be the one who told anyone in a book about writing that publication wasn't important, or to hush and eat your spinach.

I believe there are two places in which the writer lives: there is first and foremost the home that is writing itself, and then there is the house that is the pursuit of publication. There are of course other elements of the writer's life—coffee figures in prominently, as well as the age-old dilemma of pen or pencil, or the new worries (at least, new in my lifetime as a writer) over which font to use. These and other complexities of the writer's life must be confronted, but for the purposes of this essay I'm keeping to what I feel most comfortable addressing.

And here's what I know most intimately, and most truly, about the life of a writer: You will be rejected. Period.

As David sang of the coming Messiah in Psalm 118—"The stone the builders rejected has become the capstone"—so too will the fact of rejection itself be the capstone of your publishing life. I truly believe that dealing with rejection—indeed, embracing it—will be the make-or-break factor in one's life as a publishing writer. Rejection is the firm foundation as well as the house that is one's pursuit of publication; the publications themselves will be the art upon the walls, while the house itself—the nails and boards and Sheetrock and shingles, and of necessity the sweat and tears and hammered thumbs with which all of these are erected—will ever and always be your own story of how you weathered the rejection that is sure to come upon your work.

I also want to say that building your house of rejection—placing the capstone that is your embracing of this inescapable truth of trying to publish—is predicated fully on the presumption that the work itself is the best you can possibly make it, and that you have been moved to write not by a will toward fame or fortune or even posterity, but because the work of writing is good work, and the reward inherent to writing is the writing itself. To quote again from Mr. Carver's essay "On Writing," "If the writing can't be made as good as it is within us to make it, then why do it? In the end, the satisfaction of having done our best, and the proof of that labor, is the one thing we can take into the grave." I am certain he wasn't talking about tossing into your coffin with you your published works as being the proof of that labor, but rather the element of character wrought in you with producing a written work that means something, that gave you something you didn't know before, that enlarged your world somehow and provided a place of rest or warmth or understanding for the shivering and anxious human being you are. The element of your character that writing to the best of your ability brings about in you will be something that will be remembered by those you love long after you are dead and gone, and long after the journals in which you published have moldered away into nothing.

One more caveat before we get going: neither is the house that is the pursuit of publication even a necessary shelter. That is, publication is not needed, if one writes because one writes. Here is Brenda Ueland once more on finally seeing why she wrote, "At last I understood that writing was this: an impulse to share with other people a feeling or truth that I myself had. Not to preach to them, but to give it to them, if they cared to hear it. If they did not—fine." Here, then, is a writer who has utterly and simply and fully embraced rejection. It doesn't matter if someone else doesn't care to hear it. What matters is the feeling or truth one experiences in the writing, a feeling or truth so deep as to give one the impulse to share it. You must first write, and write well. You must first inhabit the home that is writing before presuming to hang on nonexistent walls the paintings that are your published works. Granted, the home that is the act of writing is most often—at least in my experience—nothing more than a troubled lean-to pitched in a dark woods; nevertheless, it's the woods I love, and want to explore, and that frighten me and feed me and keep me certain of how little I really do know about the way the world works, and that keep me humbled in the face of how small I really am in the uncharted forest the world of words really is.

But sometimes, if I am blessed, I wake up there in the woods to find that the lean-to I've been sleeping in is really a tree house with a magnificent view of a spectacular sunrise I hadn't imagined I might see, but secretly hoped I would all the same.

It is then, and only then, once you've glimpsed that vista, and once you have been moved by it clearly and wholly enough to try and write that vision out in a poem or story or essay or novel, and once you have been moved enough by it to want to share it, that you ought to allow yourself out of those woods, and into that house made of rejection.

Because you will be rejected. Period.

I say all this because I myself have firsthand knowledge of rejection. Just before sitting down to write this out, I counted up my rejections—I have saved every one I have ever received, except for one (there will be more on that later)—and found that there are 597 of them. These are only for stories and essays; as near as I can tell, there are another 35 or so for the books I've written. And given that I have thus far published 40 stories and 23 essays, I think I have a pretty good average: right at 1 essay or story published for every 10 rejections.

Now, I know that there will be some readers of this news who may have more rejections than me, and I want to say Hooray! because you are well on your way to, or may even have already arrived at, accepting rejection. But please do not think that I say I have as many rejections as I do to begin some sort of comparing of scars; and as for those of you who think 597 is a lot of rejections, don't believe I am saying here that I'm stronger than you, or that you have to be like me and count them all up, keep them at the ready. No. The purpose of this essay is simply to give a kind of tour of my own house of rejection to aid and encourage you in the building of your own.

My first rejection came back in 1981 when I was still an undergrad at Cal State Long Beach. I'd taken a couple of creative writing classes—I hadn't even yet declared an English major—and saw a poster asking for submissions to the student literary magazine, *Riprap*. The rejection was a terse little thing, the edges of the slip itself crooked, this as a result, I imagine, of the student staff printing out a dozen or so rejections per single sheet of paper and then cutting them with scissors into plenty enough to go around. Two sentences was all it was, but two that dug deep to the heart: I'd been rejected. And then, as if that weren't enough, I got in the mail an official rejection from the chair of the department of English, this on university letterhead, so that my first foray into publishing was a double dose of No.

This began, however, my own naïve way in which I dealt long ago with rejection: when later that semester the issue of the journal came out, I noticed that the masthead for the journal read pretty much the same as the table of contents, and I rationalized that the journal was itself a club, the editors selecting themselves, cutting out of the herd of creative writing students any lame horses they spotted. The result was that they themselves were the only steeds on the property.

Of course this logic will only get you so far, as eventually one starts to send stories to journals that live outside the rarified, even incestuous, world of a college campus. I started sending out my first stories to real journals my senior year in college, though I know in retrospect that the work wasn't much worth publishing. Still, I wanted to have a go at it, and purchased a copy of

Writers' Market, an annually published reference book that serves as something of a blue guide to journals everywhere.

The list is seemingly endless, the entries there at best confusing to a young writer who knows nothing of the author names used like poker chips of prestige to give a description of who publishes whom. Because of this, and because I had no idea you might have a strategy to publishing, I sent out stories willy-nilly, even receiving in the same week a rejection from such an august place as *The Atlantic Monthly* and a journal that, when I'd sent my story to them, had been called *In a Nutshell,* but which when it was returned came with a rejection slip that had the title of the journal crossed out and handwritten above it the word *Hibiscus.* All of which is to say, I had no clue what I was doing, where I was sending, what I hoped to achieve in even publishing anything. Even I, a snot-nosed undergrad, knew that if within days of each other I got a note back from *The Atlantic Monthly* and one back from a journal that had changed its name—there was even an emendation of the subscription rates on the back, with $12 crossed out, and above it $7—that there must have been a better way to do this.

But I didn't know what way that could be, and merely continued sending out, and getting rejected by everything from *Esquire* to *Pig Iron,* the latter being home of the most condescending rejection slip in the world at that time. The slip is smaller than most, maybe three inches by four, and depicts a version of a Monopoly game board set in Youngstown, Ohio (home of the journal), complete with smokestacks at the steel mills. Over that is a hand—mine, I guess—holding what is either a Community Chest or Chance card drawn, ostensibly, from the game board. On the card is a picture of the little Monopoly guy, hands in his pockets and looking oppressed, above him a hand giving the thumbs-down sign, beside him the words, "We regret that we cannot use your submission to PIG IRON. Go back to typewriter. Try again." I imagine that, at some point in some editor's life, that seemed quite funny and innovative, but the result of receiving that one was that I never sent them a story again. It seemed in the sense of humor the editor was trying to employ there was an inherent bent toward ridicule; the thumbs-down, the "Try again" made this endeavor seem only some sort of game, the writer the loser, the Fates that ruled the draw of the cards—the editors, of course—finally and cavalierly in power.

Yet the fact remains that publishing is, in its own way, a kind of game, but one that, it has always seemed to me, ought not involve ridiculing those to whom a journal owes everything: its contributors, those folks who are, often as not, also its subscribers. Part and parcel with that sense of ridicule is also a sense of arrogance that can sometimes bleed through the ink of a rejection slip.

Case in point: pretty early on I sent a story to *California Quarterly*, the publication of the English department at UC Davis. Although I received this time actual human response to my story with the one sentence, handwritten, on a full sheet of the journal's letterhead, a sentence that summarily weighed my story and found it wanting, giving no reason or request to see something else, it was the signature beneath it that gave me to know this was an editor to whom I did not want to submit. I kid you not, the signature measured, from top to bottom, five and a half inches, and seven inches end to end, thereby vastly eclipsing the sentence that had discounted fully my own story.

Maybe this was my own vanity itself speaking in me, but I

remember thinking, *Nope. I don't have to deal with that one,* and simply crossed it off my list of possible journals.

But what sort of a list did I, in fact, even have? How is it that I could have been willing to knock a possible venue out of my life without knowing what the heck my list *was*?

And why didn't I *have* a list?

Still I trudged along, sending to *Redbook* and *The New Yorker* at the same time I was sending to *WIND/Literary Journal* and *Rock Bottom* (nothing wrong with either of these latter journals, but they aren't *The New Yorker*). And it was at this time, too, that I got accepted to grad school, Melanie and I packing everything up and moving three thousand miles east, from Los Angeles to Amherst, Massachusetts, home of UMass, the only M.F.A. program out of the four I applied to that let me in.

Not long after arriving, too, I'd wangled my way into reading the slushpile for *Ploughshares* in Cambridge. Editor Dewitt Henry was so hard up for volunteer help he took my friend and fellow M.F.A. student Holly Robinson's word and let me cart home from Boston to Northampton once a month a cardboard box of manuscripts. I can remember sitting back on the sofa in the two-room apartment we lived in back then, half of the second floor of a Victorian at Sunset and Prospect, and reading very seriously manuscripts mailed from wannabe writers, allowing myself the highbrow thrill of thinking, *I am a writer,* because I was smart enough and talented enough and savvy enough to have been allowed to read and judge the work of others for one of the best literary journals out there.

I was twenty-two years old.

That entire fall I read around a thousand manuscripts, and passed on to Dewitt one that I thought he might like. He didn't.

Yet even now, looking back on what I myself was writing back then, I am still amazed I even got into UMass, the one program that accepted me. A sentiment, it was obvious after my first few at-bats in my first workshop, shared by pretty much everyone in class.

I was eviscerated, to say the least. Flayed alive might be a better way to put it. Or so it felt at the time.

And the awful quality of my writing wasn't a view held only by the other students, my peers. It was one shared as well by the professor himself, so much so that, at the end of my first semester in grad school, after having moved all those miles from home and taking out student loans to pay for it all, I was summoned to a "special meeting" by the professor himself. Me. Alone.

At this meeting he proceeded to give me an opinion that cut so deep that the words have been etched into my brain, still vivid and alive all these years later. "Bret," he said, and leaned toward me from his desk, me across from him in the hardwood chair against the wall, "I see no reason why you shouldn't be in our program, but I see no reason why you should."

As you may well imagine, I was devastated. I don't remember anything about that meeting past those words in his office, only that it was nighttime, after our last workshop, the window behind him black. This was December in New England, a land suddenly more alien to me than ever I would have imagined, the sun long gone, before me the lonesome ten-mile drive from Amherst back to Northampton, and those empty back roads that lined the empty fields that had, so short a time before, been filled with the bright and odd joy of pumpkins.

Somehow I made it back to our apartment, where tearfully I told Melanie we were going to leave this place and head back to California, where I would be able to get back my job as a reporter for *The Daily Commercial News,* the job I'd left in order to try and become a writer here in this godforsaken land called Massachusetts.

Thankfully, Melanie's cooler head prevailed. "We moved all the way out here," she said, "and we'll finish this first year here. Then we'll figure out if we want to go."

It was a decision that proved the turning point in my life as a writer. Which is to say, Melanie is the real hero in all this.

Because something happened after that night, and on into and through the winter break and spring semester.

This: I started to begin to get a glimmer of a glimpse of what it might mean to learn how to write.

Looking back here and now, and writing this all out for you, it's a lot easier to piece together what happened that winter break and spring, the culmination and amalgamation and whatever else you may want to call the strange brew of events and attitudes and emotions and coldhearted examinations and ruminations and observations that finally, finally resulted in my beginning—truly, *beginning*—to see how to write. It's easy here and now to see what went on, but back then . . . back then, I was living through it. Which is exactly the only way anyone can ever arrive at seeing how to write.

Those words given to me by my professor proved an integral part of that catalytic brew, a concoction that also counted as an ingredient the reading of all those manuscripts for *Ploughshares.* For months I had been looking at story after story after story, none of which, if I may be so bold, was any good. But it wasn't the lack of quality in the stories that I suddenly saw as the sad thing about the endeavor, that attempt through the services of the U.S. Postal Service to find a home for a story one had written.

Rather, it was the fact that all of these people writing all of these poorly written stories all wanted to be *published*. They all seemed only to want to get into print, rather than to have written with excellence.

And I—the reader of the slushpile, the arrogant and still snot-nosed student—was no better or worse than any of them. I wanted, in my sending stories out myself, to get published. Even the name I sent my stories out under, the name I typed on all the stories I handed in for workshop, wasn't even the name I went by, but what I thought of as a writerly version of my full name: R. Bretley Lott, the *R* for Robert, my first name (and yes, Bretley is my real middle name, derived not from Mark Twain's Western Slope writer compatriot Bret Harte, as most people assume, but from James Garner's character on *Maverick,* the number six television show in the fall of 1958). Although no one in my entire life had ever called me Robert, much less R—I was Bret from day one—still I penned each story as though I were R. Bretley, imagining as I wrote those stories (dare I admit this?) what the name would look like in the italicized font *The New Yorker* printed the author's name in at the end of a story.

Flannery O'Connor wrote in "The Nature and Aim of Fiction" that most people who write "are more interested in being a writer than in writing. They are interested in seeing their names at the top of something printed, it matters not what." This, I realized once I'd been kicked in the face with the fact of my being neither here nor there, neither fish nor fowl, neither good enough to be in the M.F.A. program nor bad enough to get kicked out, was who I was: one of the people in the slushpile, wanting only to be heard, to see my name in print.

But there was one last ingredient to that concoction that came together that winter of 1981 and 1982, one last element I needed to discover before I would begin to get that glimmer of a glimpse.

That winter I picked up a copy of Raymond Carver's short-story collection *What We Talk About When We Talk About Love*.

A copy of that book remains on my desk to this day, as I write this. That's how much of an impact the stories had on me.

I won't go any further in my love for his stories, and my admiration for the man. If you don't know who he is, suffice it to say that when he died in 1988, *The Times* of London ran a headline that read AMERICA'S CHEKHOV DIES. Suffice it to say, too, that one of the great regrets, if that is the word, of my writer's life is that, although I was blessed enough to have met him a couple of times, and to have had him read a few of my stories and to have exchanged a few letters and to have gotten him to sign his books for me, I was never a member of that hallowed group of people who knew him closely enough to call him Ray.

To say I revere his work, then, and to have kept that book on my desk, is about as close as I can get to letting you know how important he was to me, even though I didn't really know him. I met him, he was an acquaintance, he gave me my copy of Gardner's *On Becoming a Novelist*.

But he also taught me in a way I had never been taught before.

That winter, I read these stories of his, and saw real people in real circumstances, the author nowhere in sight. This may sound dumb, but before that, once I'd started to write my own stories, I thought a story was about the author's abilities to put words together, the author's insight into the human condition, the author's *talent*.

I thought a short story was a showcase for the author.

Me: R. Bretley Lott.

But here, here were stories about people in dire circumstances. Real people, starkly rendered, clearly and cleanly rendered, people who were dealing, whether they knew it or ignored it, with matters of life and death.

And nowhere, nowhere could you find the author. There were only these people, and how they would or wouldn't play the hand they'd been dealt.

In my stories, the author—me—served more as a ringmaster calling attention with a megaphone to the people I was writing about, rather than serving simply, as Carver did, as the conduit through which the story passed.

Scales fell from my eyes.

That winter break, because of this series of events—the reading of hundreds of lousy stories, the solid and stone-cold rejection of my own by a professor who told me that it remained to be seen whether or not I was worth the space I took up in his classroom, and these crystalline stories—I did two things: first, I stopped sending stories out, ceased seeking publication altogether; and second, I sat down and wrote what I consider my first short story.

It was a story that began in truth, in an incident from my childhood back in Southern California, an incident that involved my older brother, Brad, and me and our babysitter, Charlotte. It began in what really happened, and then departed, took off on its own to arrive at a place I hadn't imagined it might until I arrived there.

That is, the story told me what it was going to do. I was only along for the ride, merely writing down what I saw happening as it was happening.

I was, finally, *humbled* by the story.

I'd quit trying to build that house of rejection, quit trying to hang nonexistent art on its walls, and had gone out to the woods and that troubled lean-to that is the writing itself. Where I should have been all along.

And when I finished that story—it took most of the month of January—I realized the spring semester would be starting up in a day or two, the last semester I might spend here in Massachusetts if things went as they had last fall, and so I prepared the manuscript for workshop, typed it up one last time.

I rolled the first page into the typewriter, and began dutifully to type what I always did in the upper-right-hand corner: my name and address.

But this time it was different. This time, *I* was different.

I typed *Bret Lott* at the top of the page.

I was writing in this essay about trying to get a strategy for sending stories out, about the need for a list, before I went off on the tear these last few pages have been. Telling the story of *R. Bretley* versus *Bret* wasn't something I'd planned on telling. It's not a very edifying tale, and seems more embarrassing than anything else.

But now it seems like the most logical tale I could have told, given that this essay is about rejection. Because what finally happened in all that was that *I* and my preconceived notions about writing and being a writer had been rejected outright, first by my professor, and then—rightfully so—by me.

Typing my name that way remains, to this day, to this minute, to and through and beyond the writing of this very sentence for the book you hold in your hands, the seminal moment in my writing life. The absolute moment of reckoning myself with me.

That professor gave me about the best news I could have gotten: either one means to write and write well, or one doesn't. As I said earlier, trying to publish is predicated fully on the presumption that the work itself is the best you can possibly make it, and that you have been moved to write not by a will toward fame or fortune or even posterity, but because the work of writing is good work, and the reward inherent to writing is the writing itself.

I had to learn that lesson on my own, with the help of a professor, hundreds of wannabe writers, Mr. Carver, and my wife, who wouldn't let me quit.

Then I began to learn to write, and kept writing, and writing, and writing. And suddenly, suddenly, the stories began to get better, to be more about themselves, to be *true*.

The professor that next semester, Tamas Aczel, encouraged me, saw something in the work, beginning with that story by Bret Lott about two brothers and a babysitter; and the next semester Jay Neugeboren, who would eventually become my mentor, my guide, my literary guardian angel, my editor nonpareil, seemed to enjoy what I had written for him as well.

So: we didn't leave.

And I didn't start sending stories out right away.

Because now I was taking this whole thing seriously, and I figured out, finally, how to send stories out.

I read, simple as that. We were blessed enough to have lived in a town that had three independent bookstores, all of which carried a good assortment of literary magazines, and though I couldn't afford to buy a lot of them, I started to hang around a great deal more at those bookstores, perusing, grazing, touching, holding those journals.

If you aren't fortunate enough to have a bookstore near you that carries more than a couple of journals, then you must do the extra legwork of finding them on your own, either in the periodicals at your local public or college library, or by writing or e-mailing journals and buying, usually at a discounted price, sample copies of the ones you're interested in. But you must do this work—this *research*—so that you can begin to figure out which journals are well produced, which feature authors whose work you admire, which are established and don't look like they'll be changing names or cutting rates anytime soon. What you are looking for, ultimately, is which journals you would be proud to be in.

For most of that year, in addition to learning how to write, I worked at making my list of which places I wanted to be in, because, now that I had had those scales fall from my eyes about what it meant to write, I didn't want my work to appear just anywhere. I know that sounds pretentious, but why, I reasoned, would I want work that is as good as I can make it to appear just anywhere? Why would I start at the bottom and try to work my way *up*?

There is a hierarchy, dear readers. Some journals are better than others. Some are the best. Some are places in which I wouldn't want my grocery list to appear.

But you must develop that list, and *you must not sell yourself short.* Stories get into print in a journal once, except on rare occasions; that one place in which that story or poem or essay appears ought to be a place you will be satisfied to have had it appear.

By that fall, I had a list of about forty places, beginning with *The Atlantic,* next *The New Yorker,* and moving on from there.

(And no, I won't here give you that list, as every list will be different, and will depend upon your own tastes and desires. Get your own list!) I typed that list up, and taped it to the wall above my desk. Then I began a log of where I was going to send which story, a sheet of blank paper upon which I drew four columns top to bottom, at the top of the first column the word *What* (for the name of the story), on the next column *Where* (for which journal I was sending it to), then *When* (the date I would send it out), and, cleverly, *Well . . .* (when that story would arrive back at my mailbox).

Then I went to the local stationery store, bought a bundle of nine-by-twelve-inch manila envelopes, a fresh ream of paper, sheets of address labels, and a postage scale. Next I went to the post office itself, and bought an array of stamps. Of course all of this was at that time in our lives as graduate students a great and luxurious expenditure—there were weeks sometimes when we had lots and lots of Kraft macaroni and cheese and Spam for dinner—but it was an expenditure that was necessary: this was a serious endeavor, this publishing, now that I had started to write seriously.

What happened, then, was that the act of seeking publication became a kind of cottage industry: I had my postal scale, my stamps, all the paper products I could need; I had my agenda (I wrote at the top of that first log sheet AGENDA, and did on each of the next twenty-three sheets I filled up, even call it that now on the file I keep on my computer); and, finally, I had my stories.

I had my stories.

That October, I finally put things into gear, and taped on the wall next to that list of journals the agenda. I went to the local copy store—this was before the computer printer, mind you, the

advent of which has proved to writers an immeasurable blessing, one unimaginable twenty-five years ago—and had several
copies of each of the stories I planned to send out made. I went
home, typed up the address labels—two return addresses for
every one journal address—and then typed up the cover letters
for each submission, making certain that those letters were
written to the correct and current editor, so that the journal
would know I had done some research. Addressing a submission
to a particular person shows that you care enough about that
journal to have found out who runs the thing, thereby showing
as well that you are, again, taking this whole thing seriously.

They were cover letters that spoke of no recent publications,
no writerly honors, nothing. I had none of those. They merely
read, "Enclosed please find the story _____, which I hope
you will enjoy and consider for publication. Thank you for your
time and attention, and I look forward to hearing from you."
Simple as that. No explanation of the story, no intriguing details
about me, no Day-Glo stationery, no pleading, no juggling, nothing.

Because I saw this for what it was: a business transaction.
This was a profession. Not the *writing*—please don't mistake me
for saying that *the moment of creation* is a business transaction.
Remember: that's the lean-to in the woods, a place you go because you love to be out there. But the building of the other
house is a *profession* in the largest sense of the word: you are
making a statement of faith—a *profession*—that what you have
written is good, and worthy, and true.

I decided too that I would submit my stories multiply, once
they had worked their way through the upper echelon of journals I wanted to be in, unless, of course, a journal said some-

where in its masthead that it didn't take multiple submissions. Then I was honor-bound not to do that. It seemed back then, though less so now, that multiply submitting a story was an unethical thing, that somehow you were obliged only to show a piece of writing to one person at a time.

But I decided to send out stories to several places at once because of the math involved: on average, a submission will come back to you in six to eight weeks (although I have waited over a year more than once). That means a story you have written, if it is sent to one editor at a time and once you factor in that most journals don't accept manuscripts during the summer months, will be read by only five or six people a year.

I decided that I didn't have that time. One day I would in fact die, I knew, and the stories I wanted heard mattered more to me than to the editors involved, editors who, I know for a fact, sometimes lose manuscripts, leave them in the trunk of their car or out in the rain on their deck, or inadvertently let one drop behind a desk only to find it six months later, when the furniture is being moved.

These stories were mine, and needed to be let out into the light of the printed page. But not so that I could see my name in print. No. Rather, these stories were about people I cared about, and because it was always and only me who cared most about these people, it was my responsibility to see them through to their proper lives: the written word gets published.

And to settle once and for all this matter of multiple submissions, even though I know I am getting ahead of myself, the worst-case scenario of what could happen when you multiply submit is that two journals might accept the same story at the same time—a problem everyone should have: two places want a story you have written. It's a risk you run, and though it may mean that you have burned a bridge by turning down an offer to publish your work by one journal over another, rest assured that there are many, many bridges out there.

I have had this happen four times altogether, the acceptance of a manuscript by two journals at once. The decision about which one to allow to publish my story was easy: whoever responded first. Period. I have never encountered any hard feelings from the editors who were a little late in asking for the story—in fact, every journal I had to say no to subsequently published another story I sent them.

And so, almost a year after I'd stopped sending them out, and almost a year after I'd begun to get a glimmer of a glimpse of how to begin to learn to write—almost a year after I'd been *humbled*—I began again to submit, carefully and lovingly and coldly logging in on the agenda where I'd sent what.

Then I went back to the blank sheets of paper, and wrote more stories, and more, and more. Because that was home: those woods.

And of course, this was when the rejections began in earnest. Looking back through the pages of the agenda, I can see that there are dates when two and three rejections came back in one day, and strings of three and four and even five days in a row when I received No for an answer.

Though I'd be lying to tell you that the rejections didn't hurt—every one of them did, I assure you—there was in me then the assurance and confidence that I was on the right track, that I was doing this the best way I knew to do it. One of the perks that came along with multiply submitting, I soon found out, was that I really couldn't be thinking of what was going on with my stories once they were out of my hands. This was because there were simply too many to enumerate in my mind—my record for the most things out in the mail at one time stands at twenty-four, four stories out at six places apiece—with the result being that rejections simply became a part of the daily mail, just the routine. And because I wasn't thinking of *one* story out to *one* place, I had freed up my head to concentrate as fully as possible on *the next story I was writing.*

Don't get me wrong: I have never been able to be nonchalant about what I have sent out in the mail. I love the mail, wait for it every day; when I am out of town, I talk to Melanie two or three times a day, and inevitably I will work the conversation around to what we got in the mail, secretly waiting for some bit of some good news about something I have out in the mail. I don't ask what came in the mail to get a list of catalogs or which bills have shown up. But I listen patiently, as a good husband should, and then, if there's nothing about writing in that list, I'll say, "That's it?" still hoping, hoping there has been some nugget overlooked, an acceptance, or a rejection.

And I know good and well that Melanie is onto me. She knows I'm addicted to the U.S. Mail.

But having all those stories out in the mail meant that rejection became a part of my life, and as a means to accommodate myself to that fact I came up with another facet to the strategy: once a story was out in circulation, once I'd done the best I could possibly do and had decided to put it up for public consumption, I decided that that story would, to the best of my ability, never spend another night under my roof.

Our mail came in the morning back then, and so I had in hand the bad news of the day early on. All that remained for me to do was to go to the agenda, log in the date the story had been returned, look down the list of which journals either had some-thing of mine or didn't, and then decide where I would send that story. All I had to do was type up that cover letter and address label, then assemble the self-addressed stamped envelope and letter and story—I had that postal scale and my supply of stamps—and then later that day I would walk or drive down to the post office and give that story what had by that time become the optimistic and yet realistic send-off into the mail slot: I hoped it wouldn't come back to me, but knew most likely it would.

And come back they did, like leaves off a tree all year round. You don't get 597 of them without working at it.

There were the little squares of beige paper *The North American Review* sent, and the bright yellow squares *The Georgia Review* gave out too. *The Southern Review* used green paper that re-minded me of Milk of Magnesia, while *The Antioch Review* used a heavier, more dignified card stock, a pale yellow slip that still said No.

The Paris Review sent out plain white paper: all business, those people. But, like my hierarchy of journals, they had their own hierarchy of rejection slips, a fact it took a few submissions to finally recognize.

The bottom-of-the-barrel rejection they sent out was one that said sternly thank you, but no. The next step up was one that said no, but that let you know that they thought your work was interesting. Finally, there was the rejection that said although they were turning you down, they wanted to see more.

The crowning moment of my relationship with *The Paris Review* came when, having run their gauntlet of rejection slips, I received a personal letter from one of their editors, an encourag-ing note that let me know they had read it but declined.

So close, so close. But I never got in there.

But, as with that letter from *The Paris Review,* there began to come back, from all my salvos into the blue, human responses on those slips, from the single word "Sorry" scribbled on the bottom of one from *The North American Review* to the series of scrawled but encouraging missives from Jim Schley at *New England Review/ Bread Loaf Quarterly* through to letters—*actual letters!*—I got back from Michael Curtis at *The Atlantic* and Dan Menaker at *The New Yorker.*

For many years I sent every story I wrote first to Michael Curtis and then to Dan Menaker—as far as I can tell I stopped sending after twenty-seven stories, when my commitments to novels eclipsed my desire to write stories, and also because I realized I just wasn't going to get into those two august places— and I received back from them both, not counting the time or two they were on vacation, a letter for every story. I have never been published in either magazine, but looking back I find it really, truly doesn't seem to matter. What mattered was that I was being taken seriously enough by these two editors to have my work commented on, to have given to me in return for my story the time out of their lives to type a letter to me (or to have had a letter typed) to say an encouraging word or two.

This was an immeasurable gift, and still is: whenever you receive a rejection that has even the smallest scratch of a word on it, count it all good, as editors are in no way obliged to comment, and given the volume of manuscripts that comes to most good journals, to make a reader even pause long enough to put pen to paper, even if to say No, is nothing short of a triumph.

Sometimes, though, you can get a message that isn't so encouraging, such as the time I got a testy note back from Peter Stitt, editor of *The Gettysburg Review,* who took me to task for how I had behaved toward my younger son, Jacob, in an essay I had written and sent to him. In the note he mentioned nothing about the quality of the essay, but about the imbecility of me, and how yelling at Jacob about how he had to love his brother was quite detrimental to the boy.

At first, I was taken aback by what he'd written: that was, as far as I could tell, the *point* of the essay: I was the fool at the center of my own life. But then I realized that something wonderful had actually happened in his sending the story back: I had touched on something in him, made him feel deeply something about me and about my son. The essay, I saw, actually worked.

Rather than revise the essay or toss it away, I immediately sent him another essay, another one about Jacob, and in my cover letter told him that I hoped he wouldn't hold the last submission against me, and hoped as well he'd enjoy this next one.

He took it, and ran it as the first piece in the issue.

The original essay I sent him, that one that touched a nerve? I sent it right away to *The Iowa Review,* who took it.

Another testy letter came about as the result of a multiple submission. A story I'd sent out to several places at once was taken by a journal, and it was then my responsibility to write the others and ask for the story back. An editor at one of the journals sent the story back with an angry letter berating me for sending it multiply, though there was in none of its available information any language that said you could not do so. The journal later published another story I sent them.

But the worst rejection I ever got—the only one I have ever thrown away—was from none other than Gordon Lish, the infamous editor who first put Raymond Carver on the map by publishing a story of his in *Esquire* back in the seventies, and who subsequently became the editor of Mr. Carver's early books.

Back then, Gordon Lish was an editor who could make or

break a career—or so it seemed to many. He was known for publishing new talent—writers whose work was "strenuously literary," as he put it—and he was responsible, to one degree or another, for the literary careers of many important writers. Chief among them Raymond Carver.

He also edited a journal, *The Quarterly*. It was cool, so cool that pretty much everyone I knew who was sending stories out wanted to be in there. Never mind that the preprinted rejection slip that came back with your work was 416 words long, one long held-breath of cloying prose on one fourth of a standard piece of paper. It was an annoying rejection, pseudo-self-deprecating and oh-so-sensitive; one passage actually reads "I hope you will be persuaded to trust certain assurances—namely, that I am abundantly glad to have your notice, that The Quarterly would be pointless without your continuing favor. . . ."

But that preprinted rejection wasn't the one I threw away. No, the only rejection I ever threw away came from the hand of Gordon Lish himself, a slip of paper with one sentence scrawled across it: "This is so derived of Carver it hurts." Beneath it were the initials G.L.

I wadded it up, threw it in the kitchen trash, I was so angry. Then I pulled it out of the trash, read it again, staring at the summary statement that cut to the bone. What an idiot this man was! I was trying to learn all I *could* from Raymond Carver, the one from whom I had learned so much about what it meant to *write*. Who was Lish to say such a dismissive thing to somebody trying so hard to *learn* from Mr. Carver?

And so I wadded it up again, threw it in the kitchen trash again. This time, I left it there.

But then I got out the story, and looked at it. I looked at it, and looked at it. And though it took a few days—this was one time when I let the story spend a few more nights at home—I began to see that, indeed, the story *was* derived from Carver.

I rewrote it, made it wholly my own. The first place I sent it, *The Michigan Quarterly Review,* one of the best journals in the country, took it.

Which is all to say, even the worst rejection I ever got taught me something.

But let's go back for a last few moments to that October in 1982, when I'd sent out my first stories after that hiatus from seeking to see my name in print.

It's a good place to return, because it was the real beginning of this long tale of reckoning with what will always be a part of your writing life: rejection.

And here's proof it will always be so: last week—today is August 7, 2004—I got a rejection from a journal. Number 597. Back in April I decided to send out what I had so far written of my next novel, and mailed three sections of it to three journals (I don't multiply submit anymore). About the middle of July I got an e-mail from *The Georgia Review* saying they wanted the section I'd sent them; a week later *The Gettysburg Review* e-mailed to say that they were taking the section I had sent them as well.

Which left the last journal, *Virginia Quarterly Review,* from whom I heard last week. No, they said.

The lesson? Even with nine books published, you will still be rejected.

But I didn't know all that back on an October day nearly twenty-five years ago. Back then, there was only my stories, this list of journals, these envelopes and labels and letters and stamps.

There was only the future.

And it came, in the flush of all those colorful rejections.

But one day early that next year—January 16, 1983, I can see right here on my agenda—I got a letter.

I get the chills even now—really—as I write this, thinking about that moment when I opened an envelope addressed to me from Clackamas Community College. No place I'd ever been.

Inside it was a letter from Craig Lesley, then fiction editor for *Writers Forum,* a journal published annually at the University of Colorado, Colorado Springs. I'd sent a story I'd written the summer before, a seven-page thing that had taken me an entire week of living down at Melanie's parents' summer cottage on Barnegat Bay to write. I'd had big plans to write a hundred pages of fiction when I'd set off from Massachusetts to the Jersey shore, but had only emerged with that one little story. "That Close," it was called, about an argument between a husband and wife, and a drive the husband takes afterward, believing he has won the fight. It had already been turned down six times.

"Dear Bret," the letter began. "Happy New Year with some good news!"

The letter was an acceptance.

Craig told me in the letter that Alex Blackburn, the editor of the journal, would be sending me an official letter in a few days to thank me for the story. Then he wrote, "One change: Alex suggests a better title would be 'The Man Who Owned Vermont' and wants to publish it as such."

It was an acceptance.

I called Melanie at work over at Neuroscience and Behavior

at UMass; she cried on the phone, and brought me flowers home that evening. That evening, too, we celebrated by going out to dinner to Carbur's, a somewhat fancy restaurant, at least to us grad students, where we spent a grand total of forty dollars, a gigantic sum for us back then. And I wasn't even going to get paid for the story, instead would only receive five free copies of the journal.

But it didn't matter. It was an acceptance.

Perhaps this may all seem to place an inordinate emphasis on the literary journals. Perhaps you are thinking all of this fuss over obscure periodicals is somehow just not important enough for you to worry over. That you've got bigger fish to fry than to hammer away at a literary journal.

But let me finish for you this long tale of the building of my house of rejection.

Later that spring another acceptance would come, this one from *The Iowa Review,* the letter written by an editorial assistant on behalf of the editor, James Alan McPherson; the issue my story, "This Plumber," would appear in was going to be a special issue called "One Hundred Years After Huck: Fiction by Men in America." That story had been turned down seven times before being taken.

A few months after that another story, "Open House," was taken by *The Yale Review.* This one had been turned down eight times.

All this while rejections of other stories still rained down.

Then one day in 1984, a few months after we'd moved from Massachusetts to Ohio—and a few months after that fateful evening when I'd been watching *Dallas*—I got a letter from a woman named Debra Spark, a student in the writing program at Iowa who was trying to put together an anthology of short fiction by young writers. *Thirty Under Thirty,* it was to be called, as it would be a collection of thirty stories by writers under age thirty. She wanted to know if she might use my story "This Plumber"—she had read it in a recent issue of *The Iowa Review*—for the anthology. Go right ahead, I wrote her back, and although I was flattered, I remember thinking, *That doesn't sound like something I'll hear about again.*

One day in early 1985, me about two thirds of the way through that first novel, I got a letter in the mail from one Nat Sobel. He was a literary agent, the letter said, and he had read a story of mine that had recently appeared in *The Yale Review,* a journal to which he subscribed. Was I working on a novel, and could he see it in the hopes of representing me?

I thought it was a scam, but did some research, found out immediately that he was the real thing. And so I called him to talk to him. Though I was still a hundred pages or so from the end, I told him about the novel, and about the fact that four pieces of it had already appeared in the literary journals, including the story he'd read in *The Yale Review.* "Send it to me," he said, and six weeks later I got a call from my agent, Marian Young, who was working for Nat Sobel back then. "We'll take it," she said, "but first you have to finish it."

I spent the next few months finishing it, and found in the mail one day another letter from this Debra Spark. The anthology was now called *Twenty Under Thirty*—she hadn't been able to find thirty stories she liked—and there had been a few nibbles but no bites on the sale of her book yet.

Interesting, I thought, and went back to the novel, finishing it in August 1985. That was when Marian began to send it out, and when the rejections began. They piled up pretty quickly, and by Christmas we had eight.

But other good news had come along: Debra Spark had sold the anthology to Scribner's, which would be publishing the book that next April, and I would see the story I'd originally published in one of those journals in the pages of a real-live book. I also had to sign my first real-live contract with a publishing house, and actually got paid $200 for the story. Pretty good for a short story I'd already published once.

And still rejections came.

Then in May 1986, *Twenty Under Thirty* was reviewed in *The New York Times Book Review*. It was a terrific write-up, and though Phillip Lopate, the reviewer of the book, spent most of his space on three or four stories other than mine, he did make mention of "This Plumber" and graciously said a few kind words about it.

By this time we had accrued twelve rejections of the novel, all from large publishing houses. Marian's thirteenth try was Viking, and I nearly laughed when she told me she was sending it to such an important house. Viking? Right.

Melanie and I had planned to visit her parents in New Jersey for her mother's birthday, and because I'd not yet met Marian— we'd handled all our business by mail or phone—I asked her if I might be able to come into the city and meet her once we'd arrived and settled in at Melanie's parents. Sure, she said, come on in for lunch.

The drive to New Jersey from Ohio, we decided, would be broken into two parts, with a stay at a hotel somewhere in Pennsylvania. We had both boys by then, Zeb having just turned three, Jacob only five months old. Once all four of us went to bed in that hotel room in Carlyle, Pennsylvania, Jacob, overwrought from all that time in the car—or perhaps out of pure orneriness—decided to scream all night long. Really.

When we finally rode into Matawan, New Jersey, around eleven that next morning, we were all of us blitzed, burned to the ground. But I had this lunch date with Marian, and so after dropping off Melanie and the boys I drove to the train station, got on board, and rode into Manhattan.

I walked from the Port Authority all the way to Nat Sobel's offices on Fourteenth Street not because I wanted the exercise, but because I really didn't know what we were going to talk about over lunch, and I needed yet more time to figure out what to say. All I could think about was the fact the novel had been turned down twelve times. How could we talk about that, and expect to eat lunch too?

But however empty of conversation I was, however burntout from the traveling and no sleep, I still made it to the office, a townhouse on a shady street, and knocked on the door, and finally met Marian Young.

She brought me back to her office, sat me down in a chair beside her desk, then smiled, said, "We had an offer. This morning. Viking."

I stood up, I sat down, I shouted, I turned around. "Praise God!" I said, and sat down and stood up again. "Can I hug you?" I asked her, because I needed to hug somebody, and Melanie wasn't there. "Sure," Marian said, then laughed, stood up from her desk, let me hug her.

It had happened, today. Now. Here was Marian Young, telling me this.

The editor, she went on to tell me once I had sat down again, and once I had begun to breathe, had read Lopate's review, recognized my name in the review as being the name of the author of the novel on her desk, and had taken it home, read it, and now had made an offer.

It had happened.

But it had only happened—and here is the crux of this entire essay on rejection—*because the stories and that novel had been sent out, had been rejected, and then sent out again and again.* The four stories that ended up appearing in my first novel had been rejected, altogether, a total of twenty-eight times; that finished novel had been turned down twelve. And every one of those rejections had to have been received before those stories and that novel could arrive in the hands of an editor who would take it.

One of those stories showed up in a journal that an agent happened to subscribe to, and led to my being taken on as a client.

One of those stories showed up in a journal that an enterprising and inspired young anthologist read, that person choosing to include my story in a book that gained notice in the most important newspaper in the world, notice that was seen by an editor who happened to have on her desk the novel represented by the agent who happened to subscribe to the journal that happened to print my story.

And one of those stories was the first to have ever seen publication, the editor there seeing in the few pages I'd sent him the title this whole story needed: *The Man Who Owned Vermont.*

My first book.

I have written in another chapter in this book on the issue of why one even writes to begin with that, once I have written the story, I want to publish it, and that this is the way things ought to be: you have a story, and you want it to be heard.

But I also said in that chapter that you must not believe that the hearing of your story—the publishing of it—is the end, that publishing will be the central monument to your life, or that it will bring you a kind of joy that has eluded you all your life. Publishing is, again, its own reward, but it is the joy of having written that story that is the truest reward.

And finally, I want to go back to that verse from Psalm 118, "The stone the builders rejected has become the capstone." The next verse reads as follows: "The Lord has done this, and it is marvelous in our eyes." That is, rejection is a thing of marvel. One is putting one's heart out for public consumption, that public a cold and cruel world with little room for the luxury of broadcasting your heart, no matter how small that listening world really is. Pursuing publication requires something very near bravery coupled with a kind of brazen humility—they don't call it a submission for nothing.

But most necessary, even more important than bravery and humility, a characteristic inextricable to the process of writing and publishing both, is the element of tenacity, of steadfast stubbornness and dogged perseverance; imperative as well is the element of faith—that's the title of the last chapter in Gardner's *On Becoming a Novelist*—that what you have found in that lean-to of yours out in the woods is worth hanging on the walls of that house built of rejection.

But first spend the requisite retreat in that lean-to in the woods; find in the writing what you can take to the grave—that satisfaction in having done your best. And then, and only then, embrace rejection. Marvel at it; build that house. Take no for an answer, and then ask again and ask again and still again, until finally the answer is yes.

The Ironic Stance and
the Law of Diminishing Returns

· ·

PART ONE,

*in which the beloved Wife spurs on the Author to cite Opaque Examples
of what he thinks he Means*

"What do you mean by irony?" my wife says to me, the two of us
in the bathroom, her leaning in to the mirror over the sink and
taking out a contact. I've followed her in here from the bedroom
at the end of this day, trying to tell her what the heck this essay
is about as a kind of warm-up to actually writing it, because I'm
still not sure what I mean, and I still haven't written it, and I'm
starting to get scared. I'm trying it out on her, in the hopes she
might give me some sort of gesture of confidence, some sign she
believes in me, that I can do this.

"Irony," I say. "You know, irony. Like, irony." I say all these
words with a kind of authority, using my hands held out in front
of me, palms open, as if this gesture will in itself bring meaning.

She finishes with one eye, the contact there on the tip of her
finger, and turns to me. She gives me the smallest shake of her
head. She narrows her eyes at me, and I know I am in focus and
out at the same time.

She says, "What are you talking about?"

And so, in her honor and because I am no dummy, this confession:

Now that I'm actually sitting down to try to write this out, I don't even want to do it.

Because what do I know? A particular aesthetic, to begin with. The kind I like to write, and like to read. I begin with my prejudices—sometimes the only really true possessions we can claim as our own. So that's where I begin this talk on irony and its uses and overuses and misuses and all that.

My prejudices for and against.

So, where does that leave me? Why is it I wanted to talk about this topic to begin with, and what the heck is this topic anyway? What possessed me to think I had anything to say?

What is irony to begin with, and why, in my prejudiced opinion, is its overuse, its having become the language we speak, its being the very air we breathe the root of a problem facing the contemporary narrative form?

What I mean by the law of diminishing returns and the ironic stance is this:

Every time I see the bumper sticker QUESTION AUTHORITY!, I want to ask the owner of the vehicle, *Who are you to tell me what to do?*

Thus fulfilling his directive to empower myself, and in the same instant nullifying his authority to do so. We are both left, as a consequence, nowhere and with nothing.

There. That sums it up quite nicely.

Or, maybe, this will work:

My student comes into the office, winded as they all are at

the climb up here, three flights to the attic of this old Victorian in the center of campus. The last flight is up a narrow staircase that shoots like a ladder to my office door, the door cut at an angle to allow for the pitch of the roof, so that in addition to the climb my students must also duckwalk past the threshold, then emerge into a room with a wonderful dormer that leads out onto the roof, a room with pitched ceilings plenty high enough to let them stand in, the short walls lined with books and more books.

Because of all this, I have the best office on campus: the students who come to see me want to come to see me.

Lee is one of them. He wants to be a writer, wants to be one with all his heart. He's told me this plenty of times while sitting up there in that office, the two of us talking about what it means to write and to be a writer.

I believe him. He wants to be writer.

Today we're going to talk about a story he dropped off in my mailbox downstairs last week. Even though his face is flushed from the climb up here, I can see as he finally stands up straight in the room that he knows this one didn't work. I can see it in the way he's already smiling, slowly shaking his head at me. He takes off his backpack, sets it in one of the two chairs opposite my desk, then sinks into the other. He stops grinning, looks at the carpet, then at the desk edge before him, then at me. Then he grins again.

I say, "What's wrong?" though I know precisely.

He says, "There's just no heart to it."

I reach out to the desktop, pick up a paper clip and tap it, quietly, on the blotter. I say, "Why do you say that?" and now I am grinning too, because he and I both know. This is the third story he's turned in this semester with just the same problem.

"Yeah, yeah," he says. He shoots out a breath, seems to sink even lower into the chair. He's grinning even bigger now, slowly shaking his head. "I know exactly why," he says. He says, "I'm not happy with it."

"Why?" I say, tapping the paper clip. His bookbag is partway open on the chair beside him, and I can see in there copies of *Libra* and *White Noise*. Texts for the DeLillo special topics course he's taking.

Don DeLillo: his favorite writer this semester.

He shakes his head one more time and, so chagrined it's as though he's confessing to a crime, he says, "I'm just so afraid of being cheesy."

Let's try this one on:

A couple of years ago I was a visiting writer at a low-residency M.F.A. program where I gave a lecture on creative nonfiction. The lecture included several passages regarding my two children, and made reference to my love for my wife; in it I confessed to knowing nothing about writing, and that this not knowing was in fact my own key to trying to understand it all. Later that day I gave a reading of a personal essay, in which I was revealed to be the fool at the center of my own life, a recurring theme in pretty much all of my essays.

But an odd thing persisted that day, while I spoke to people, while I shook hands after the reading, while I fielded questions after the lecture: I couldn't read the crowd. I couldn't gauge how I was doing, many of the students stone-faced, reticent, it seemed. Reserved at, and in, my presence.

Then, the next morning at breakfast in the cafeteria, a woman came up to me at my table, where I was eating alone.

Still as stone-faced as most everyone had been the entire day before, she said to me, "Several of the women in our program were talking last night." Her hands were together in front of her, her mouth a straight line. It seemed what she wanted to say was taking some effort, as though this was work. "Your lecture and the essay made you sound like a sensitive person. As though you knew what you were talking about." She paused, nodded at her words, her eyebrows together in what seemed a kind of bestowal of something important upon me.

I nodded, smiled, a little appreciative, a little apprehensive. "Thank you," I said.

"We decided that we believe you," she said then. "What you said about writing, and your sensitivity. We just wanted you to know we believe you." She nodded again, the bestowal accomplished.

"Thank you," I said, and I know I blinked a couple of times too many. "I'm flattered," I said, and smiled, nodded myself, blinked one or two more times.

I'd been believed through democracy. They had voted, and reached a consensus: the visiting writer really did know nothing. And their decision to believe so was a gift to me, they wanted me to know.

The woman gave a final, quick smile, then went to her table, where she sat down among several other women to finish her breakfast.

I still blink a couple times too many when I think of that morning, that breakfast, that belief reached by ballot.

PART TWO,

or The Law of Diminishing Returns (The tendency for a continuing application of effort or skill toward a particular project or goal to decline in effectiveness after a certain level of result has been achieved)

"Irony," a Hollywood mogul once said, "is what goes over the heads of the audience."

Its etymological pedigree goes back to the Greek *eiron,* which means dissembler, or one who disguises or conceals behind a false appearance. The most famous dissembler, of course, was Socrates. In Plato's *Apology,* Socrates testifies to his systematically alienating everyone who is said to have wisdom by asking each a series of leading questions designed, according to Socrates, to find someone wiser than himself in order to disprove the oracle at Delphi's pronouncement that Socrates was indeed the wisest. Unfortunately for Socrates, these questions revealed to him that he in fact was the wisest, and that "the men most in repute were all but the most foolish; and that some inferior men were really wiser and better."

It's no wonder, then, that the ire he raised with all those important people he'd shown to be fools resulted in his death; his apology—his defense—didn't do anything to help, and one can see in Plato's study the crankily humble Socrates heaping further coals on the heads of the fools around him. The result is, of course, Socratic irony, or the art of dissembling to teach others humility. Or, according to Webster's, "a pretense of ignorance and of willingness to learn from another assumed in order to make the other's false conceptions conspicuous by adroit questioning."

The dissemblee, though, saw all this differently. One student of Plato's, Tyrtamus, left his tutelage for Plato's greatest rival, Aristotle, who subsequently named him Theophrastos, or "divine speaker." Theo (if I may) was the first to synthesize and survey the beliefs and notions and philosophies of his predecessors, and in the following assessment of irony, written sometime around 300 B.C., we can see clearly the kind of bitterness engen-

dered by the dissemblers in those who have been, as it were, So-
cratically ironized (one can almost see here as well the specter of
a proto–Jerry Seinfeld):

> Irony, to comprehend it in a brief definition, is a misrep-
> resentation for the worse in word and deed. The ironical
> man is he who approaches his enemies and desires to
> have talk with them and let all hatred cease. He praises
> people to their faces, and behind their backs inveighs
> against them, but when they lose lawsuits bewails their
> fate with them. . . . Never does he admit that he is doing
> anything: he is always considering. He will pretend he is
> just this moment come, or he was late or he has been ill.
> To borrowers or those calling for a subscription he gives a
> large sum and says he is not rich. When he has something
> for sale he says he never sells, and when he does not wish
> to sell declares he will. He will hear but pretend he did
> not, or see and say he never saw. If he has admitted some-
> thing he declares he has forgotten all about it. He will
> say he will see about it or sometimes has no knowledge
> whatever, or again is quite amazed, or perhaps he had
> thought so, had he not? His habit in short is to be using
> this sort of phrase, "I don't believe it," "I can't follow," "I
> am thunderstruck," "You say he has changed from what
> he was," "That's not what he said to me," "The thing is ab-
> surd," "Tell that to someone else," "I am at a loss whether
> to disbelieve you or blame him," "Now beware of trusting
> too quickly." Such are the phrases, such the windings and
> turnings of which the ironical man makes use. Men so
> double and designing in character are more to be guarded
> against than serpents.

This, I believe, is the definition of irony by those whose pretense and arrogance have been revealed by the dissembler and who are still sore about it; thus Plato's definition of the end result of Socratic irony—"The greatest level of wisdom man can hope to attain is the realization of how little he knows"—was being abused even as far back as 300 B.C., resulting in men who were dissemblers for their own purposes, whether defensive or political or, like Seinfeld, purely for entertainment.

But there are further definitions of irony, further curlicues and eddies and tendrils that have evolved through the eons; this, again, from Webster's:

> **2 a :** the use of words to express something other than and esp. the opposite of the literal meaning **b:** a usu. humorous or sardonic literary style or form characterized by irony **c:** an ironic expression or utterance
> **3 a** (1): incongruity between the actual result of a sequence of events and the normal or expected result (2): an event or result marked by such incongruity **b:** incongruity between a situation developed in a drama and the accompanying words or actions that is understood by the audience but not by the characters in the play—called also *dramatic irony, tragic irony*

There's also the venerable Fowler's take on the subject in his *Dictionary of Modern English Usage:*

> Irony is a form of utterance that postulates a double audience, consisting of one party that hearing shall hear and shall not understand, and another party that, when more is meant than meets the ear, is aware both of that more and of the outsiders' incomprehension.

But what happens when the party that is aware both of that more and the outsider's incomprehension becomes unable to extract himself from that cold-blooded cocoon of detachment that knowing all this can become?

What happens when, a couple of millennia later, once Freud enters the picture, and we are suddenly and irrevocably shackled to self-consciousness, all of us made to believe our emotions are generic, our dreams predictable, our neuroses placable, our imaginations hardwired to nothing more than our fear of death and predilection for sex?

Freud "taught us to analyze [our feelings], which turned us into the objects of our own dissection," wrote the novelist and short story writer Roxana Robinson in *The New York Times Book Review*. "The idea of passionate engagement came to seem naive and foolish as we moved from an innocent, 19th-century, pre-Freudian childhood to a 20th-century adulthood, detached and analytical."

What happens when art, like science (included in the latter the new psychoanalysis), finds modernity its siren call? The term *modern* meant, until quite recently, common, voguish—what was not to be emulated, as it had no depth or purpose beyond its own presence as something "new." In 1506, when Michelangelo was a young man and ancient Rome was still being excavated and rediscovered, the statue *Laocoön* was uncovered and paraded through the streets as being a fantastic revelation of pure beauty, and even though Michelangelo had already sculpted what was to be his own most enduring and beautiful work of art, the *Pietà,* he was so genuinely moved by the dynamic emotion caught in *Laocoön* that, later in life, he went on record as saying he'd staked his entire artistic life on that particular statue, finished in the second century and lost for so many hundreds of years. The Pre-Raphaelite Brotherhood, in reaction to the industrialization of England, founded their own school on the artistic integrity of artists dead and buried for hundreds of years.

But it wasn't until the mid-nineteenth century that the term *modern* was accepted as a critical term, one that could be applied in a benevolent way to the creation of art. Jacques Barzun, in his monumental and indispensable history *From Dawn to Decadence: 500 Years of Western Cultural Life, 1500 to the Present,* writes of the outbreak of Modern,

> Thanks to this changed view of modernity, art joined science in spreading the 20C dogma that latest is best. Modernist Man looks forward, a born future-ist, thus reversing the old presumption about ancestral wisdom and the value of prudent conservation. It follows that whatever is old is obsolete, wrong, dull, or all three. . . .
>
> Philistines were still alive and kicking late in the Cubist Decade [1900–1910]; they disappeared into the trenches with everybody else. By 1920 any that survived had been miraculously transformed, not into aesthetes but into trimmers and cowards. To this new breed anything offered as art merited automatic respect and gave scrutiny. If a new work or style was not easy to like, if it was painful to behold, revolting, even, it was nonetheless "interesting." Half a century later unless the reviewer finds it "unsettling," "disturbing," "cruel," "perverse," it is written off as "academic," not merely uninteresting but contemptible.

And what happens when the Great War turns out to be only the first one, and the Second turns out to have been a kind of fragmentation bomb that leads to an array of wars and rumors of wars still blossoming around us to this day?

What happens when news becomes an element of our every waking moment, and politicians—liberal and conservative both—break apart words and their meanings before our very eyes and ears, no matter the smile all the while or the stern set of the jaw?

What happens when, now, a student walks up to you and says he's afraid of being cheesy, when what he means to say is, *I'm afraid of writing about love?*

What else can one do, other than deconstruct bumper stickers, stand fearfully outside of that ring that demarks one's heart open to the world, and wait to believe until you've consulted others?

Where else can our hearts be save for hidden away in the cloak of our stance, our distance from others, our fear of appearing—oh fate worse than death!—*impassioned?*

In the remarkable book *For Common Things: Irony, Trust and Commitment in America Today,* Jedediah Purdy, a twenty-six-year-old wunderkind, writes:

> Our leading cultural currency today is a version of the stubbornly flat skepticism that Tocqueville observed. We practice a form of irony insistently doubtful of the qualities that would make us take another person seriously: the integrity of personality, sincere motivation, the idea that opinions are more than symptoms of fear or desire. We are wary of hope, because we see little that can support it. Believing in nothing much, especially not in people, is a point of vague pride, and conviction can seem embarrassingly naive. . . . Irony is powered by a suspicion that everything is derivative. It generates a way of passing

judgment—or placing bets—on what kinds of hope the world will support. . . . What do we find so untrustworthy that we dare put such scant weight on it? We surely mistrust our own capacity to bear disappointment. So far as we are ironists, we are determined not to be made suckers. The great fear of the ironist is being caught out having staked a good part of his all on a false hope—personal, political, or both.

I would here have to add artistic hope; that is, we don't want to be caught out having hope in art.

And as if to validate such a truth as this—that we don't want to be caught out having hope—another wunderkind has appeared on our literary scene almost simultaneously with Purdy's work. Dave Eggers's memoir, *A Heartbreaking Work of Staggering Genius,* is a book that purports to tell the tale of twenty-two-year-old Dave himself whose parents both have died, leaving him to raise his kid brother, for the most part, alone. It's an interesting book, one that has been critically acclaimed for its innovative form (though that pretty much peters out fifty or sixty pages in). The following shows us that he is a dissembler, and that such forethought and fore-forethought about his outward appearance dictates an ironic stance:

> We are wearing what we always wear, shorts and T-shirts, having decided, after thinking about what to wear and then remembering not to think about what to wear, to wear what we would have worn had we not been thinking about what to wear. We are happy with our shorts and T-shirts, one side tucked in, just an inch of it on the right side, showing some belt, the rest hanging out—this is our look—it having been arrived at in high school

through careful consideration, through the eschewing of so many possible mistakes.

And yet the hallmark, it seems, of those adopting so fully and cavalierly the ironic stance seems to be a wild and raucous backing away from even that term, as though being caught out even having a stance were some form of commitment, commitment being the worst word one can use upon the Ironical Man. The following passage on the author's hatred of irony is from the appendix to *AHWOSG* that accompanies the paperback version— an innovative (sort of) and entertaining (sort of) cluster of pages and words that do nothing more than defend the young man's hardback edition from any misreadings by the idiot masses; it is, finally, a rebuttal to anyone who might have had critical points to make about the book. He writes,

> You can't know how much it pains me to even have that word, the one beginning with i and ending in y, in this book. It is not a word I like to see, anywhere, much less type onto my own pages. It is beyond a doubt the most over-used and under-understood word we currently have. I have that i-word here only to make clear what was clear to, by my estimation, about 99.9% of original hardcover readers of this book: that there is almost no irony, whatsoever, within its covers. But to hear a few people tell it, this entire book, or most of it, was/is ironic. . . .

What follows is a lengthy definition of irony, in smaller and smaller and smaller typeface and of course posed in the words generated by the author, to defend himself against the perceived attack calling something ironic is seen to be in this, our post-ironic age.

No, *post-ironic* doesn't mean irony is dead, despite the assertions by our prevalent ironists that it is. Rather, as with the term *postmodern*—"a theory based on the belief that there can be no such thing as a single, or even a properly privileged point of view," to quote Mary Warnock in *Imagination and Time*, "the 'I' who was central to Kantian theory, who constructed the world according to a priori laws has, it is argued, had its day, along with the laws themselves"—the post-ironic posits that we have gone beyond irony to a simple recognition of the absurd as our everyday, as our language, as the air we breathe.

Irony, it turns out if you believe in not believing anything at all, has been dissembled.

Part Three,
in which the Author Breaks Out into a Sermon, Dammit!

So, I want to ask, is any of this news?

No. Art has reiterated the ironic, has dissembled and dissembled and dissembled humans in order both to entertain and instruct from day one.

A Sumerian proverb goes like this: "Build like a lord, live like a servant. Build like a servant, live like a lord." In these few and ancient words the hollowness of human ambitions and desires is revealed all at once.

In Gerald Bullett's novel *The Jury*, published in 1935, we find this desultory passage on the self-consciousness of words:

> Every word was wrong; every word was Romantic, banal, probably used by the so-called poets of the 19th Century. He tried again: ochrecous [*sic*] residue, heart's dregs— that was sufficiently unlike Tennyson, but it wouldn't do. Heart was one of the bad old words. But why write about

autumn at all—another prohibited word. It all shows how second-rate I am, he concluded.

And Thomas Frank, author of *The Conquest of Cool* and the editor of that engagingly contentious journal *The Baffler,* has observed in *Harper's,* "[S]o widespread has the ironic impulse become that the only thing about irony that really startles anymore is its longevity as an American style."

So, if none of this is anything new, what's missing? What are we to do in order to make our stories—our hearts—new?

We must, I believe, see that irony is in and of itself only a tool of illumination, and not the subject of what is to be illuminated. It's as though we have finally arrived at a time when, no longer believing there can be a path out of the cave we are living in, we have become content to use the flashlight of irony simply to cast hand shadows—this one is *sarcasm,* this one *hypocrisy,* this next one *facetiousness,* and this one *ridicule*—across the walls of the craggy and wet darkness in which we believe we have no choice but to reside, instead of using the flashlight—this tool that can and does reveal our folly as human beings—to limn a path out.

The poet Richard Hugo, writing in *The Triggering Town,* yet another book any artist needs to own, confesses to the folly of contemporary literature's self-consciousness by noting that

> all art that has endured has a quality we call schmaltz or corn. Our reaction against the sentimentality embodied in Victorian and post-Victorian writing was so resolute writers came to believe that the further from sentimentality we got, the truer the art. That was a mistake. As Bill Kittredge, my colleague who teaches fiction writing, has

pointed out: if you are not risking sentimentality, you are not close to your inner self.

And in what has proven to be a prophetic vision of this age of the Internet and the promise of a worldwide web of connections between human beings but which has resulted in the further cloistering of us all, our faces lit not with the light of another human soul but with the faint glow of our computer monitors, Charlie Chaplin's monologue at the end of *The Great Dictator* speaks as well to what pointless ends our cleverness—our ironic stance—will take us:

> I should like to help everyone if possible, Jew, gentile, black man, white. We all want to help one another, human beings are like that.
>
> We all want to live by each other's happiness, not by each other's misery. . . . In this world there is room for everyone and the earth is rich and can provide for everyone.
>
> The way of life can be free and beautiful.
>
> But we have lost the way.
>
> Greed has poisoned men's souls—has barricaded the world with hate; has goose-stepped us into misery and bloodshed. We have developed speed but we have shut ourselves in: machinery that gives abundance has left us in want. Our knowledge has made us cynical, our cleverness hard and unkind. We think too much and feel too little: more than machinery we need humanity; more than cleverness we need kindness and gentleness.

My text this morning is from the Gospel of Mark, and so if you would please turn with me to—

Sorry—I forgot. This isn't a sermon, though I know it sounds like one. But I'm not kidding about the Gospel of Mark being our text. In Chapter 10, John Mark tells the story of Jesus and the rich young ruler, the brief moment of their meeting. He writes:

As Jesus started on his way, a man ran up to him and fell on his knees before him. "Good teacher," he asked, "what must I do to inherit eternal life?"

"Why do you call me good?" Jesus answered. "No one is good—except God alone. You know the commandments: Do not murder, do not commit adultery, do not steal, do not give false testimony, do not defraud, honor your father and mother."

"Teacher," he declared, "all these I have kept since I was a boy."

Jesus looked at him and loved him. "One thing you lack," he said. "Go, sell everything you have and give to the poor, and you will have treasure in heaven. Then come, follow me."

At this the man's face fell. He went away sad, because he had great wealth. Jesus looked around and said to his disciples, "How hard it is for the rich to enter the kingdom of God." The disciples were amazed at his words. But Jesus said again, "Children, how hard it is to enter the kingdom of God. It is easier for a camel to go through the eye of a needle than for a rich man to enter the kingdom of God." The disciples were even more amazed, and said to each other, "Who then can be saved?" Jesus looked at them and said, "With man this is impossible, but not with God; all things are possible with God."

There. Perhaps one of the most widely known passages in the Bible, especially that last part about the camel through the eye of the needle. But what makes this story so memorable, so important and vital—if you believe in Heaven and Hell—and yet so utterly ironic? The rich young ruler has been utterly dissembled; that is, through Jesus's exacting incision into the man's soul, revealing in a moment the source of the man's identity, his pride in his possessions, all his presumptions have been put aside. The rich young ruler knows well the *technique* (there's that word again) by which living for God is found—he has kept the commandments since he was a boy!—but when faced with how *faith* is found, through the ultimate surrender of self and the consequent following of Christ without a clue where that might lead, the young man comes up short, for his identity as a man of God has been based on the technique of being a man of God, and not on the surrendering fully of the self the world tells us is of value.

It's not so much his earthly possessions but the way he's allowed them to distance himself from his fellow humans that keeps him from being the man of God Jesus sees him as capable of being. The wealth he has acquired while keeping the commandments is inextricably entwined with his notion of what being a man of God is, and it is Jesus who sees this mistaken notion, this chasm between the rich young ruler and those in need around him. Jesus knows and tries to get the young man to see that communion with God—eternal life—is not accomplished by the cleverness of attending to rules or the accumulation of material wealth. Communion with God is accomplished through loving others.

An irony that goes right over the heads of the audience, his disciples.

But Jesus isn't merely a Socratic ironist. He's not feigning ignorance as a means simply to reveal folly in others, or to refute what some oracle has said about him, though the news of who he was at his birth was enough to make the reigning Hebrew monarch and Roman puppet slaughter every Jewish boy under the age of two.

No, Jesus was different from any other ironist, though irony was his means so very often of explaining and illustrating and teaching and living. The difference here is that Jesus, in revealing the rich young ruler, "looked at him and loved him." And it is this love that is missing from the way in which irony is now being employed.

Jesus knows the earnestness of the man's heart, knows his desire is true, but knows too it is a desire based on the notion there is a way that can be found, if one only follows the rules closely enough. Jesus loves him, I believe, because he sees the truth that he may very well have followed the commandments since he was a boy. But it is that step away from self-conciousness and into grace that is the core and truth of salvation—and, I believe, the core and truth of the making of art—and it is a step the young man cannot make. And, finally, Jesus assuages his disciples—us—with the element of hope: "With man this is impossible, but not with God; all things are possible with God."

Irony's necessary partners, then, are hope and love.

But how, you might well ask, do we attain the power to find hope in our work?

Here is J. D. Salinger, in "Seymour: An Introduction," one of the most powerful passages that I have ever read on how we might find purpose and meaning inside what we do as writers. It's a definition that bears no resemblance whatsoever to any sort of ironic stance one can adopt; it is, in fact, so bereft of any sense of irony that its sincerity, earnestness, and honesty nearly shout, and might even seem to some, well, cheesy.

Seymour writes to his younger brother Buddy, a struggling writer:

> When was writing ever your profession? It's never been anything but your religion. Never. I'm a little over-excited now. Since it's your religion, do you know what you will be asked when you die? But let me tell you first what you won't be asked. You won't be asked if you were working on a wonderful, moving piece of writing when you died. You won't be asked if it was long or short, sad or funny, published or unpublished. You won't be asked if you were in good or bad form while you were working on it. You won't even be asked if it was the one piece of writing you would have been working on if you had known your time would be up when it was finished. . . . I'm so sure you'll get asked only two questions. *Were most of your stars out? Were you busy writing your heart out?* If only you knew how easy it would be for you to say yes to both questions. If only you'd remember before ever you sit down to write that you've been a reader long before you were ever a writer. You simply fix that fact in your mind, then sit very still and ask yourself, as a reader, what piece of writing in all the world Buddy Glass would most want to read if he had his heart's choice. The next step is terrible, but so simple I can hardly believe it as I write it. You just sit down shamelessly and write the thing yourself. I won't even underline that. It's too important to be underlined. Oh, dare to do it, Buddy! Trust your heart.

And although my understanding of the human heart is first that it is untrustworthy—"The heart is deceitful above all things and beyond cure. Who can understand it?" Jeremiah writes—my other understanding of the human heart, the understanding that saves me and allows me as a writer to, in fact, write from my heart just as Seymour exhorts Buddy Glass, is the truth of God's care to make whole that which is incurable. "I will give you a new heart and put a new spirit in you; I will remove from you your heart of stone and give you a heart of flesh," God speaks in Ezekiel, and it is only in residing in this promise, my old clever life surrendered, the new and alien one here inside me, that I have been able to trust my heart, and try to find hope in the act of writing.

David Foster Wallace, author of *Infinite Jest,* the ironist's ironist's ironist's novel, another wunderkind considered one of the premier new writers of our time, though merely the literary progeny of the dangerously chuckling Mr. Stanley Fish—this is a topic large enough for an entirely new essay!—writes in an article that appeared in *Review of Contemporary Fiction,* on television and the American novel:

> The next real literary "rebels" in this country might well emerge as some weird bunch of anti-rebels . . . who have the childish gall actually to endorse and instantiate single-entendre principles. . . . Too sincere. Clearly repressed. Backward, quaint, naïve, anachronistic. Maybe that'll be the point.

It's a strange passage for such a writer as him to pen, for inside these few words lurks an almost wistful longing, as though he himself, the point man for the post-ironic age, finds himself alone in the trench and dreaming of liberation, of a day when he might be allowed to taste cool water, see blue sky and green hills.

But as for his notion of who the next rebels might be, I'm banking on his being right. The radical move right now is to have hope, to look out at the world in love in order to discover it anew in whatever way you can, in whatever form you can—please note, this essay has not entertained even a moment's derision of metafiction—risking all the while cheese, corn, schmaltz.

The radical move right now is to infuse our post-ironic age with hope, and with love, risking, as it always and ever should be, your own heart.

The Most Fragile Book

I used to be a Boy Scout. I camped in the mountains and forests and deserts of Arizona until I was sixteen. Then my father was transferred to grimy, overcrowded Los Angeles. I wanted to be a forest ranger. But the forestry program I'd attended in my freshman year at Northern Arizona University had less to do with nature than with producing future executives for Weyerhauser and Georgia-Pacific.

I went back home and enrolled at Cal State Long Beach. I became a marine biology major. Then I got a D in a physics course I needed at least a C in. I quit college, became an RC Cola salesman for no good reason other than that was what my father had been. I figured it was a way to make money. Maybe it was the career I'd been headed for all along. I knew RC Cola inside and out.

But after a year of selling soda pop, I felt like a phony. Every time I walked into a grocery store to talk some phony into buying a phony product no one really needed, I found myself longing for college and a life that perhaps might have meaning beyond the claustrophobic world of all these phonies around me.

I had Tuesday nights free, and the only class with an opening at my local community college was Creative Writing. I signed up for it.

The teacher was a wild-haired, Harley-riding poet/professor from Cal State, while here I sat at my desk, just off work and in my RC uniform, the wide blue tie with the swirly red and white logo at the very tip, the navy blue polyester work pants, the black leather steel-toed shoes.

Everyone else in the class was in civilian attire, and more than once the poet/prof looked at me in my uniform and smirked, slowly shook his head.

I didn't fit in.

Then one night he assigned a novel, at the name of which everyone around me beamed appreciatively. It was a book I'd never heard of.

I went home that night, in hand this novel with the oddball title, and lay on the old beat-up sofa in the front room of the house I shared with three friends, two of them surfers, the other a seminary student, and started reading this story about a kid named Holden Caulfield.

He was a good-hearted and well-meaning if a bit prickly sixteen-year-old who'd been kicked out of prep school. It's the late 1940s, New York City, and he's supposed to be heading home to his parents' apartment. But he decides instead to sort of run away, and try to live some kind of life that might make sense for as long as he can in a world infested with phonies.

I kept reading there on the sofa—and kept reading and reading and reading on through the night, reading this amazing book, this totally true book, this genuinely real book, told by Holden with an urgency and intimacy I'd never encountered before.

This was me, this Holden Caulfield. This was me, "surrounded by jerks," me and Holden both oppressed by and shackled to a life that didn't allow us any power of our own. This was me, too, "the most terrific liar you ever saw in your life," as Holden informed me he was at the start of things—I was a soda pop salesman (who in his right mind needs soda pop?); and here was me, too, dreaming about just the right girl and knowing it wasn't going to happen.

All of this was me, despite the fact Holden was there in postwar New York City and getting drinks and a hotel room and a hooker (sort of), then ice-skating innocently enough with his would-be girlfriend, Sally Hayes, at Radio City, who wears "this little blue butt-twitcher of a dress."

He was right about everything, this Holden Caulfield, even if he was a little bit brittle, psychologically speaking: the world really is full of jerks and phonies, and innocence is being stripped from us every time we turn around, and the only thing it seemed we could possibly do was to try and save someone we loved (for Holden, it was his younger sister, Phoebe), to "catch a body comin' through the rye."

This was about me, the me that'd been drifting what felt so many years, from one hope for a future to another to another—park ranger to biologist to salesman to uniformed geek in a classroom of wannabe writers, chief among them this poet/prof and his smirk.

I finished reading the book and sat up, there in the house I lived in, and suddenly I was in a different room, in a different house, on a different beat-up sofa. The world was different now.

All because of this book, this true book. This book was solid. *Right on, Holden!* I wanted to shout to the house, to my job, to that creative writing class, even if my housemates were asleep, the phonies. *Tell it like it is, Holden!*

Then, I grew older.

Eventually, I became a writer myself.

I reread *The Catcher in the Rye* four or five more times during the next several years, holding it dearer each time, admiring it more the deeper I went into my own life as a writer. It's no easy feat, let me tell you, to pull off a first-person voice as sharp and moving and quick and believable as Holden's, nor is it a simple endeavor to infuse the few days over which the story takes place with as much life and confusion and as many full-blooded characters as Salinger does.

But more important than Salinger's art was Holden's idealism: each time I reread the book I wanted nothing more than to again be Holden, still raging against the way the world wanted to swallow all of us whole.

My family had begun to grow, we moved here and there at the whim of teaching jobs, we were continually stone broke. Next-door neighbors held parties in their apartment, parties that ended up brawls in the parking lot outside our back door; student papers nagged to be graded every waking moment, the five classes of remedial English I taught sometimes feeling more a babysitting job for the semiliterate than actual teaching; rejections of my stories piled up like leaves off a tree.

And we had two children—two boys—whose presence in our lives amplified the whole notion of meaning: here were two new human beings on planet Earth, two new people whose paths had to be blazed by my wife and myself, while we ourselves were trying to blaze paths of our own.

For a few dark years, we had to put them in day care full-time, from eight in the morning until six at night, just so that we could make ends meet.

Those boys grew, and there came a day for each when he no longer wanted to hold my hand when we walked across the street, or from the car to the grocery store, or from here to anywhere.

Later still, things in my writing life took a stranger twist than I had ever dared imagine, thanks to Oprah, such that I found myself one evening not long ago sitting in a leather chair in a room we call the library in the new house we'd bought, and holding in my lap a first edition of *The Catcher in the Rye*.

It had been maybe fifteen years since I'd last reread the book. I wanted to revisit the old urgency, the old idealism, the old sense of true, of solid, of *Right on, Holden!* I'd had visited upon me the night this all began.

I wanted to see the old me. The one before leather chairs and first editions. The me that raged against all the phonies out there.

I read—and read and read and read. And here was the same old urgency, the same brash assessment of everyone and everything as phony, the same longing for love and the same desire to save the innocent.

But it was a different book this time—a better book, an even truer book, for a certain passage early on, a passage I had of course read before, but that only now revealed the length and width and depth of this young kid's, this *child's* perplexity at the fragility of life.

Here is that passage, in which Holden allows himself and us the briefest of glimpses into the inner reaches of his heart:

> I was only thirteen, and they were going to have me psychoanalyzed and all, because I broke all the windows in the garage the night he died, and I broke all the goddamn windows with my fist, just for the hell of it. I even tried to break all the windows in the station wagon we had that summer, but my hand was already broken and everything by that time, and I couldn't do it. It was a very stupid thing to do, I'll admit, but I hardly didn't even know I was doing it, and you didn't know Allie.

Allie. His brother, younger by two years, who died of leukemia when Holden was thirteen.

I sat up, there in the house I lived in, and suddenly I was in a different room, in a different house, on a different leather chair. The world was different now.

This story, I saw there in the comfy confines of the library and leather chair and adulthood, was about a child's grief, plain and simple, and in that moment too the book suddenly became infinitely larger than ever I had thought it could be. Suddenly the entire book—this passage occurs in only the fourth chapter—had cast over it a pall through which I only then realized we were to view Holden's assertions about the world. Sure, I'd known he was brittle before this; sure, I'd known his little brother had died each time I'd read the book before this. But those early readings had been filled with me, at the center of my life.

This was a book written for me yet again. Me, a parent of two children on the very edge of being grown-up themselves. How would I feel if one of my sons had died, and the other—in the

throes of his grief, in the face of the irreconcilable and incon-
solable truth that the phonies live and the innocent die—what
if he broke every window in the garage, beat on the windows of
the van until his hand was broken and bleeding?

And I loved Holden even more. But now not only for his
fierce rage against the phonies of the world, but also and even
more dearly for the fragile state from which that rage emanates:
Holden knows firsthand the black and nonreturnable gift of
grief.

When will my own sons know this gift? I was forced to wonder.

The world was different, yet again.

This is the most fragile book I have ever read. Fragile, because
in the initial rush of its ferocious beauty, the young who read
it—myself included—can see Holden as their spokesman against
the machine, yet in the same instant Holden is himself utterly
breakable, because beneath that fearless veneer bent on expos-
ing the world in all its pretension is a fearful child.

Inside that ferocious stance is a broken heart.

Now, though I still want to shout *Right on, Holden!* despite the
embarrassingly archaic sound of the rallying cry of my youth, I
also want to whisper, *Be careful, Holden.* I want to say, *Please hold
my hand.*

My older son is leaving for college, his freshman year, in
two weeks. *Be careful, Zeb,* I have resolved to say, but also *Tell it
like it is!*

And, because of this book, because of the strength of its truth—
we will all lose our innocence, and grief will come upon us—
I will also say, *Please hold my hand.*

Toward Humility

∙∙∙

5

Once it's over, you write it all down in second person, so that it doesn't sound like you who's complaining. So it doesn't sound like a complaint.

Because you have been blessed.

You have been blessed.

You have been blessed.

And still you know nothing, and still it all sounds like a complaint.

4

You are on a Learjet.

It's very nice: plush leather seats for which legroom isn't even an issue, the jet seating only six; burled wood cabinets holding beer and sodas; burled wood drawers hiding bags of chips, boxes of cookies, cans of nuts; copies of three of today's newspapers; a stereo system loaded with CDs.

Your younger son, age thirteen, is with you, invited along with the rest of your family by the publicist for the bookstore chain whose jet this is. When you and your wife and two sons pulled up to the private end of the airport in the town where you live, there on the tarmac had sat a Learjet, out of which came first the publicist, a young and pretty woman in a beige business suit, followed by the pilots, who introduced themselves with just their first names—Hal and John—and shook hands with each member of your family.

"You're all welcome to come along," the publicist had said, and you'd seen she meant it. But it was an invitation made on the spot, nothing you had planned for. And since your older son, fifteen, has a basketball tournament, and your wife has to drive, it is left to your younger son to come along.

Your younger son, the one who has set his heart and mind and soul upon being a pilot. The one whose room is plastered with posters of jets. The one who has memorized his copy of *Jane's Fighting Aircraft of World War II.*

"I guess we can get you a toothbrush," you'd said to him, and here had come a smile you knew was the real thing, his eyebrows up, mouth open, deep breaths in and out, in his eyes a joyful disbelief at this good fortune. All in a smile.

Now here you are, above clouds. In a Learjet, your son in the jump seat—leather, too—behind the cockpit, talking to Hal and John, handing them cans of Diet Coke, the publicist talking to you about who else has ridden in the corporate jet. Tom Wolfe, she tells you. Patricia Cornwell. Jimmy Carter. And a writer who was so arrogant she won't tell you his name.

This is nowhere you'd ever thought you might be. Sure, you may have hoped a book you wrote might someday become a bestseller, but it wasn't a serious hope. More like hoping to win the lottery. A pretty thought, but not a whole lot you could do about it, other than write the best you knew how.

But getting on a list wasn't why you wrote, and here, at 37,000 feet and doing 627 miles an hour over a landscape so far below you you see, really, nothing, there is in you a kind of guilt, a sense somehow you are doing something you shouldn't be doing.

Riding in a Learjet to go to a bookstore—four of them in two days—to sign copies of your book.

Your book: published eight years before, out of print for the last two. A book four books ago, one you'd thought dead and gone, the few copies left from the one and only hardcover print run available in remainder bins at book warehouses here and there around the country.

A book about your family, based on the life of your grandmother, who raised six children, five of whom were born in a log cabin your grandfather built, the last of those six a Down syndrome baby, a daughter born in a country hospital in 1943 and for whom little hope of living was held out by the doctors of the time. It is about your grandmother, and the love she has for that baby, her desire to see her live, and her own desire to fix things for her daughter as best she can, if even at the cost of her other children and, perhaps, her husband.

A book recently anointed by a celebrity talk show host. Not a celebrity, but an icon. Not an icon, but a Force. A person so powerful and influential that simply because she announced the name of your book a month ago, your book has been born again.

Bigger than you had ever imagined it might become. Bigger than you had ever allowed yourself even to dream. Even bigger than that. And bigger.

Guilt, because it seems you're some kind of impostor. Even though it is based on your family, you had to reread the novel for the first time since you last went through it, maybe nine years ago, when it was in galleys. You were so tired of it by then that, like all the other books you have published—there are eight in all—you haven't read it since. But this one you had to reread so that you could know who these characters were, know the intricate details of their lives so that if someone on the television show were to have asked you a question of an obscure moment in the whole of it all, you would have seemed to them and to the nation—Who would be watching? How many people? As many as have bought the book? And more, of course—to be on close terms with the book, with its people, its social context, and historical and spiritual significance.

You wrote it ten years ago.

And yesterday you were on this talk show host's program.

Tom Wolfe, you think. Jimmy Carter, and you realize you are dressed entirely wrong, in your dull green sweater and khaki pants, old leather shoes. Maybe you should have worn a sport coat. Maybe a tie. Definitely better shoes.

You can see the soles of your son's skateboard shoes, worn nearly through at the balls of his feet, him on his knees and as far into the cockpit as he can get. He's got on a pair of cargo shorts, the right rear pocket torn, and a green T-shirt. He'd been lucky enough to wear a fleece jacket to the airport this February morning in the sunny South.

This is all wrong.

The publicist continues on about who has ridden in the corporate jet, and you nod, wondering, *How did I get here?*

All you know is that you wrote this book, and received a phone call the first week in January, a call that came on a very bad day for you, a call that found you out a thousand miles from your home, where you were teaching others how they might learn to write. A job in addition to the daily teaching job you have so that you might make ends meet, and so that your wife wouldn't have to work as many hours as she has in the past.

The Force found you there, on a very bad day, and gave you unbelievable news. And now your book is on the lists.

You think about that day. About how very bad it was, how empty, and hollow, and how even the news that was the biggest news of your life was made small by what happened.

And now the plane begins its initial descent into the metropolis, and your son returns to the seat beside you, still with that incredulous smile, though you have been airborne nearly an hour. Hal and John happily announce you'll be landing in moments, the landscape below hurrying into view—trees, highways, cars, homes. Nothing different from the view out any airplane window you have looked before, but different all the way around.

Everything is different.

The jet settles effortlessly to the ground, taxis to the private end of an airport you've flown into before, the public terminal out your window but far, far away, and you see, there on the tarmac as the jet eases to a stop, a Mercedes limousine.

You look at your shoes, and at your son's. His cargo shorts. This sweater you have on.

"When we were here with Jimmy Carter, the lines were all the way out the store and halfway around the building," the publicist says. "This is going to be fun," she says, and smiles, stands, heads out the door past smiling, nodding Hal and John.

Then John asks, "What would you guys like for dinner?"

You and your son look at each other—he's still smiling, still smiling—and then you look to John, shrug, smile. "Subs?" you say, as if the request might be too much to manage.

"No problem," John says, and both he and Hal nod again.

Here is the store: brick, tall, a presence. A single store in a huge bookstore chain, every store complete with a coffee bar and bakery, a gift shop with coffee mugs and T-shirts and calendars.

And books.

You climb out of the limousine before the chauffeur can get around to open your door, because you don't want to make him feel like you're the kind of person who will wait for a door to be opened. Then you and your son, the publicist in the lead, make your way for the front doors.

Inside is a huge poster in a stand, the poster two feet by four feet, advertising your being at this store for a signing. In the center of the poster is your picture, formidable and serious, it seems to you. Too serious. This isn't you, you think. That person staring pensively off the photographer's left shoulder is somebody posing as an author, you think.

There are a few people in the store, and you wonder if the line will form a little later on, once the signing gets under way, and you are ushered by a smiling store manager in a red apron to the signing area.

It's in the middle of the store, and is a table stacked with copies of the anointed book, and with reprints of the earlier three books, and of the four that have come out since the anointed one first appeared all those years ago. Your books, you see, are piled everywhere. Books, and books.

"Look at this!" the manager exclaims, and points like a game show hostess to a rack of paperback books beside you, the best-seller rack. "You're the number one book," the manager says, and you see the rows of your book, beneath them a placard with "#1" printed on it.

You look at your son to see if he's as impressed as you are beginning to be.

He smiles at you, nods at the books, his eyebrows up.

He's impressed.

You take your seat behind the table laden with your books, and see between the stacks that there is a kind of runway that extends out from the front of your table to the other end of the store, a long and empty runway paved with gray blue carpet. Big, and wide, and empty. "We'll get you some coffee and cookies, if that's all right," the publicist says to you, then, to your son, "Hot chocolate sound good?" and your son says, "Yes ma'am," and "Thank you."

You are here. The signing has begun.

But there are no customers.

You wait, while the manager announces over the in-store speakers your presence, fresh from yesterday's appearance on national TV. This drives a couple of people to the runway, and they walk down the long corridor of gray blue carpet toward you. It seems it takes a long time for them to make it to you, longer even than the flight up here from your hometown, and you smile at these people coming at you: a young man, tall and lanky; a woman your age with glasses and short brown hair.

They are smiling at you.

You know them. Students of yours from the program where you teach a thousand miles from home. They are students of yours, friends, writers. Both of them.

You stand, hug them both, introduce them to your son, to the manager back from the announcement, and to the publicist returning now with that coffee and hot chocolate, those cookies.

Then the three of you remark upon the circumstance of your meeting here: they live in the same city, and have been waiting for your appearance at the store; how wonderful and strange that your book has been picked, what a blessing!; when Jimmy Carter came here, the line was out the door and halfway around the building.

You talk, sip at the coffee, don't touch the cookie. There are no other customers, and the manager promises they will come, they will come. She's had phone calls all day asking when you will get here, and if the lines will be too long to wait through.

You talk more, and more. Talk that dwindles to nothing but what is not being said: where are the customers?

Now, finally, fifteen minutes into a two-hour signing, you see an older woman rounding the end of the runway. She has bright orange hair piled high, and wears a tailored blue suit. She's pushing a stroller, and you imagine she is a grandmother out with her grandchild, the child's mother perhaps somewhere in the store right now, searching out children's books while Grandma takes care of the baby.

It's an expensive suit, you can tell as she moves closer, maybe thirty feet away now, and you see too the expensive leather bag she carries with her. The baby is still hidden under blankets, and you smile at the woman as she moves closer, closer, a customer heralding perhaps more customers, maybe even a line out the store and halfway around the building by the time this is all over.

Then here is the woman arriving at the other side of the table, and you see between the stacks she is even older than you believed. Heavy pancake makeup serves in a way that actually makes her wrinkles bigger, thicker; watery eyes are almost lost in heavy blue eye shadow; penciled-in eyebrows arch high on her forehead.

And you are smiling at this person, this customer, as she slowly bends to the stroller and says in the same moment, "Here's the famous writer, Sophie, the famous writer Mommy wants you to meet," and she lifts from inside the blankets, the woman cooing all the while and making kissing sounds now, a dog.

A rat dog, a pink bow in the thin brown fur between its pointy ears.

"Sophie," the woman says to the dog, "would you mind if Mommy lets the famous writer hold you?" and her arms stretch toward you between the stacks of your books, in her hands this dog with a pink ribbon, and without thinking you reach toward her, and now you are holding Sophie.

The dog whimpers, shivers, licks its lips too quickly, tiny eyes darting again and again away from you to Mommy.

You don't know what to say, only smile, nod, and let your own eyes dart to your students, these friends, who stand with their own smiles, eyes open perhaps a little too wide, and then you glance behind you to the publicist, whose chin is a little too high and whose mouth is open, and to the manager, who stands with her arms crossed against her red apron. She's looking at the gray blue carpet.

And here is your son. He's standing at the end of this line of people, hands behind his back, watching. He's not smiling, his mouth a straight line, and your eyes meet a moment.

He's watching.

"Sophie would love it," the woman begins, and you turn to her. She's plucked a copy of the anointed book from one of the piles, has opened it to the title page. Those watery eyes are nearly lost in the wrinkles gathering for the force of her smile. "I know Sophie would absolutely love it," she continues, "if you were to sign this copy to her."

You swallow, still smiling. "For Sophie?" you say.

The woman nods, reaches toward you for the dog, and you hand it out to her while she says, "She'll love it. She'd be so very proud."

Here is your book, open and ready to be signed.

You look at your students. Their faces are no different, still smiling. They are looking at you.

You look at the publicist, and the manager. They are both looking at you, too.

And you look to your son. He has his hands at his sides now, his mouth still that thin straight line. But his eyes have narrowed, looking at you, scrutinizing you in a way that speaks so that only you can hear, *This is what happens when you're famous?*

These are the exact words you hear from his eyes, narrowed, scrutinizing.

"She would be so very proud," the woman says, and you look to her again, Sophie up to her face now, and licking her cheek, that pancake makeup.

You pull from your shirt pocket your pen.

3

Everyone is here, your living room choked with friends, maybe fifty people in all, all there to watch the show. You and your wife have laid out platters of buffalo wings, fresh vegetables, jalapeño poppers, various cheeses and crackers and dip; there are bowls of chips, a vast array of soft drinks. Cups have been filled with store-bought ice, paper plates and napkins and utensils all spread out.

They are here for the celebration. You, on the Force's talk show, your book the feature.

Kids swirl around the house and out in the yard, their parents laughing and eating and asking what it was like to meet her, to be with her, to talk with her. Some of them tell you, too, that they have finally read your book, and tell you how wonderful your book was.

You've known most of these people for years, and there are moments that come to you while these friends tell you how wonderful your book was when you want to ask them, *Why didn't you read it when it came out eight years ago?* But you only smile, tell them all the same thing: *thank you, thank you, thank you.*

You tell them, too, that the Force was incredibly intelligent, disarming, genuine, better read than you yourself are. A genuine, genuine person.

This was what she was like when you met her, when you taped the show for three hours two weeks ago, you and her book club guests—four women, each of whom wrote a letter about the effect of your book on their lives that was convincing enough to get the producers of the show to fly them in, be these book club guests—and there were moments during that whole afternoon when, seated next to her and listening to one or another of the guests, you stole a look at her and told yourself, *That's her. That's her. I'm sitting next to her.* Moments that startled you with the reality of this all, moments that in the next moment you had to shut down for fear that thinking this way would render you wordless, strike you dumb with celebrity were the conversation to turn abruptly to you.

Then the show begins. Kids still swirl, and your wife has to pull two preschoolers from the computer in the sunroom off the living room, where they are banging two-fisted each on the keyboard, no one other than you and your wife seeming to notice this, everyone watching the television. There are no empty chairs left, no space on the sofa, the carpet in front of the TV spread with people sitting, paper plates in hand heaped with buffalo wings and jalapeño poppers and veggie sticks, and you have no choice but to stand in the back of the room, watching.

Here is what you were warned of: this episode of the book club show—your episode—happens to fall during sweeps month, when ratings are measured so as to figure how much to charge for advertising time, and since the viewership for the monthly show featuring the book and the author always plummets, the producers have decided to spend the first half of the hour with bloopers from past shows. "Forgettable moments," these fragments have been called by the promotional ads leading up to the airdate.

This was what you were warned of, two weeks ago when you were through with the taping. Officials from the show told you all this, and you'd nodded, smiling, understanding. What else was there for you to do? Demand equal time with everyone else?

No. You'd nodded, smiled, understood.

Now the Force introduces video clip after video clip of, truly, forgettable moments from past episodes: two people argue over whether the toilet paper is more efficiently utilized if rolled over the top or out from beneath; a woman tells a Viagra joke; the Force marches down the street outside her studio in protest of uncomfortable panty hose.

Your guests look at you.

"I had nothing to do with this," you say, too loud. "It'll be on the last half of the show," you say, too loud again.

They are quiet for a while, then return to ladling dip onto plates, loading up wings and poppers, pouring soda, until, finally, you are introduced, and the book, and there you are for two minutes talking about your grandmother, and your aunt with Down syndrome, your voice clear and calm, and you are amazed at how clear and calm you are there on the television, when you had wanted nothing more than to leap from the sofa you were seated on in the studio and do jumping jacks to work off the fear and trembling inside you. Now comes a series of family photos, a montage of images with your voice over it all, calm and smooth, the images on the screen pictures your family has had for years.

Pictures of your grandmother, and of your aunt.

The people you wrote about, whose lives are now here for the world to see, and you realize in this moment that you had nothing to do with this. That these photos—of your grandmother, your aunt, and your grandfather and aunts and uncles and your father too, all these family photos that have existed for years—simply bear testament to the fact they were lives lived out of your hands, and all you had to do was to write them down, getting credit for all those lives led.

You think about that bad day in January. About how this all began, and how all this credit has come to you.

Yet you are still a little steamed about losing the first half of the show, when every other author you've seen featured on the show has gotten most of the program. You are a little steamed, too, about not having some place to sit here in your living room, and about those kids banging on the keyboard. You are a little steamed.

Then the discussion with you and the four women and the Force begins, and you see, along with everyone in your house, and everyone in the country, the world, a discussion that had lasted three hours squelched down to eight minutes, and six or so of those given to a woman who gave up her Down syndrome child at birth because of the "life sentence" she saw being handed her. You see in your living room choked with your friends this woman crying over her life, her decision, and see her somehow thank you for your book and the meaning it has given her life.

You knew this would be what was included on the air. You'd known it the moment her voice wavered and cracked that afternoon two weeks ago, there in the studio. You knew it then, and now here it is: this woman, crying over giving up her baby, and thanking you for it.

And you see yourself nod on the air, looking thoughtful.

She makes great TV, you think. This woman who missed the point of your book entirely.

2

You are answering the phones for a while, because of the terrible thing that has happened this bright, cold January day.

"We'll send you a brochure," you say to someone on the other end of the line, no one you know, and as she tells you her address you do not write it down, only sit with your back to the desk, looking out the window onto the late afternoon world outside: snow, sky.

A little after lunch, this day turned very bad, a turn that has led to you here, in the office of the program in which you teach a thousand miles from home, to answer the phone for the administrative director.

She is in the other room, too much in shards to answer the phone, to field the bonehead questions that still come to a program such as this one no matter what bad things happen and when. People still call to ask about the program, about costs and applications, about credits and teachers. About all things.

Earlier today, before you began answering the phone, before lunch, your agent called here, where you are teaching others to write because it seems you know something about writing, to tell you the novel you have just finished writing is awful.

You are here for two weeks, in workshops and seminars, lectures and readings, the students adults who know what is at stake. Though they have lives away from here, just as you have your own, you and they converge on this New England campus from all over the country, the world, twice a year, to study the word and all it can mean. They come here to study writing, because they want to write, and some of them become friends to you and to the other writers teaching here, because it is this love of the word that unites you all.

Some of them become your friends.

Your agent said to you this morning, "What happened to this?" She said, "Where was your heart?"

Her call, you'd recognized with her words and tone, had not surprised you. You knew it was coming. You knew the book was dead and gone to hell in a handbasket, had known it for the last month as you'd tried to get to the end of the thing. You knew it had gone to hell in a handbasket even before you missed the deadline last week.

You knew.

The novel: a sequel to the last one you published, early last year. That one had done well, better than any of the others you've published this far. A novel you'd had a tough time trying to get published, seeing as how your books have never done that well. You're a literary author, and publishers know that means you don't sell many books. You're not a bestseller, they know. You write well enough, but you're just not a bestseller, a fact you reconciled yourself to many years ago.

But the first hardcover run of this latest book—a run in the low five figures—sold out in a few months, the publisher electing not to reprint. They'd sold as many as they'd believed they could sell, had also sold it to paperback with another publisher.

Everything was great, with selling out the print run. So great they asked ten months ago if you would write a sequel to it, and you agreed, though it wasn't anything you'd thought much about. Not until you saw how well the book was selling.

Now, here you were, ten months later, teaching people to write on a day cursed with the sad and empty curse of a startlingly blue winter sky. A day in which you have been informed of what you have known all along: this one didn't work.

You know nothing about writing.

But this is not the bad thing. It had seemed bad enough to you, walking across campus to lunch after the phone call, three hours long, from your agent, a phone call in which you both reconnoitered the train wreck before you, pieced out what was salvageable, shrugged over what was lost.

The day seemed bad enough then.

And then.

Then, after lunch, one of the students was found in his room, dead. Not one of the students, but one of your students.

Not one of your students, but a friend.

Some of them become your friends.

You were to have had dinner in town with him tonight, to talk about the novel he is writing, the novel you had been working on with him all last semester, when he was a student of yours and during which time he became a friend. A big, ambitious, strange, and haunting novel.

A novel that will go unfinished now.

He was found in his dorm room, sitting at his desk, having gone to his room the night before, students have said, complaining of a headache.

He was found sitting at his desk, reading a copy of one of your books. A novel. A lesser known one, one it seemed no one really cared for.

Your friend was reading it.

He was found at one-thirty on this blue and cursed January afternoon. Now it is four o'clock, between that time and this a somber and hushed chaos breaking out all over campus. Everyone here knows everyone here. No one has ever died here before. He was too young. He was your friend.

And now you are answering phones for the administrative director who is in the other room. You told her you wanted to answer the phone to give her time away from the bonehead questions, but you know you offered as a means to keep yourself from falling into shards of your own. You offered, so that you would have something to do, and not have to think of this very bad day, when the loss of your own book, you see, means nothing. A book means nothing.

You have lost a friend. A friend who is here, a thousand miles from home, too. A friend not much older than you, his death a complete and utter surprise. He lives with his mother, you know, where he takes care of her, an invalid, and where he is writing a big, ambitious, strange, and haunting novel.

The phone rings. You are looking out the window at the afternoon sky growing dark, the blue gone to an ashen violet, and you turn to the phone, watch it a moment as though its ringing might change how it appears, like in cartoons when the phone jumps from its place and shivers.

It rings, and nothing happens, rings again, and you pick up the receiver, hold it to your ear knowing another bonehead question is on its way.

"May I speak to _____ _____?" a man says, all business, a solid voice that carries authority with it, and you think perhaps this is an official from the college, calling on business. Not a bonehead.

"Hold on," you say, and place the phone down, go to the room next door, where she is sitting, gathering herself.

"Can you take a call?" you ask, and try to smile. "It's for you," you say, and she nods, sniffs, tries at a smile herself. She stands, and you follow her back into her office, her domain, you only a brief tenant this afternoon of a very bad day.

She picks up the phone, says, "Hello?" and her eyes go immediately to you. "You were just talking to him," she says, and hands you the phone, trying to smile.

You take the receiver, bring it to your ear, say, "Yes?"

"I'm calling from Chicago," the businessman's voice says to you, "and my boss is working on a project she needs to talk to you about. I need to break her from a meeting. Can you hold?"

A meeting, you think. My boss. What is this about?

You say, "Sure," and now music comes on the line, and you glance up at the director, who is looking at you, wondering too, you can see, what this might be about. You don't live here. You're a thousand miles from home. Who knows you are here, and why?

You shrug at her in answer to her eyes, and then the music stops with a phone connection click, and a voice you think you may recognize says your name, then her own, then shouts, "We're going to have so much fun!"

Who is this? Is this who you think it is? Is this who she says she is?

Is this her?

"Is this a joke?" you shout. "Is this for real?" And your eyes quick-jump to the director, who sits in a chair across from you, watching you in wonder.

This makes the woman calling—her—laugh, and she assures you this is no joke, this is for real, and that she has chosen a book you have written as her book of the month next month.

It's a book four books ago, a book out of print. A book about your grandmother, her Down syndrome daughter, your family.

This isn't happening. It hasn't happened. It will not happen.

But it has happened: you have been chosen. Your book has been anointed.

"This is secret," she says. "You can't tell anyone. We'll announce it in twelve days. But you can't tell anyone."

"Can I tell my wife?" you manage to get out, and she laughs, says you can, but that's all, and she talks a little more, and you talk, and you cannot believe that you are talking to her, you here a thousand miles from home and with a secret larger than any you have ever had laid upon you. Even bigger.

Yet all you can think to say to her is, *A friend of mine died today. A friend of mine died. Can I tell you a friend of mine died?*

But you do not say it. You merely talk with her, her, about things you won't be able to recall five minutes from now.

And then the phone call is over, and you hang up, look at the administrative director.

She knows who it was, you can tell. She knows, but asks, "Was it her?"

"It's a secret," you say, your words hushed for fear someone else in the office might hear. "You can't tell anyone," you say, and you are standing, and you hug her because she is the closest person to you and you have this secret inside you, and because she is the only other person on the planet to know.

You will call your wife next. You will call her and tell her of this moment, of this delivery. Of this news beyond any news you have ever gotten.

You let go the director, and see she is crying, and you are crying now, too. You are crying, and you are smiling, and you look back to the window, see the ashen violet gone to a purple so deep and so true that you know none of this is happening, none of it. This is what you finally understand is surreal, a word you have heard and used a thousand times. But now it has meaning.

A friend has died. The Force has called. The sky has gone from a cold and indifferent blue to this regal purple. A secret has been bestowed. A novel has been lost. Another gone unfinished.

This is surreal.

You go to the window, lean against the frame, your face close enough to the glass to make out the intricate filaments of ice crystals there.

You want to feel the cold on your cheek, want evidence this is real, all of this day is real. You want evidence.

You listen again to her voice on the phone, the words exchanged. You feel this cold.

A friend has died, and you did not record his passing with the Force.

And now you cry openly, watching the sky out there in its regal color, regal not for anything you have done. Only assigned that value by your eyes on this particular January day. That color has nothing to do with you, exists as it does as a kind of gift whether you are here to see it or not.

What does a book matter?

Still you cry, and do not know if it is out of sorrow or joy, and decide in the next moment it is out of both.

1

Your newest book is pretty much going to hell. In a handbasket.

Late afternoon, December, and you and your wife are in lawn chairs at the soccer field, watching your younger son play in one of the last games before Christmas.

Christmas. Your deadline for the next novel. The advance you were given, a sum the same as you were paid for your last book, even though it sold out its print run and sold to paperback as well, was spent months ago. Ancient history. Now here's Christmas coming hard at you, the novel going to hell.

Your son, a wing, is out on the field, your wife sitting beside you on your left, your older son a few feet farther to your left and in a lawn chair too, and talking to a schoolmate sitting on the grass beside him. Long shadows fall from across the field toward you, cast by the forest there. Other parents, schoolmates, brothers and sisters are spread across your side of the field, those shadows approaching you all. Maybe thirty or forty people altogether. It's a small school, new and with no field on campus, this one a municipal field at a city park. Lawn chairs is the best anyone can do.

And of course here with you, too, is your book pretty much going to hell, and this fact, its lack of momentum in your head and heart coupled with that looming deadline, might as well be a dead body propped in yet another lawn chair sitting next to you for all its palpable presence in your life. The world knows, it seems to you, that you are flailing.

You are cranky. That's what you would like to think it is. But it is more than that, and you know it, and your wife knows it, and your children do too. You are angry, resentful. You are in the last fifty pages, but the book is leaving you, not like sand through your fingers, but like ground glass swallowed down.

You believed you had something, going into the writing of it nine months ago. You believed you were headed somewhere.

You thought you knew something: that you could write this book.

So, when you see your son lag behind on a run downfield, you yell at him, "Get on the ball! Run! Get in the game!"

It's too loud, you know, with the first word out of your mouth, and you turn to your wife, say, "Why doesn't he get into the game?" as though to lend your outburst credence. As though to find in her some kind of agreement that it's your son slacking off, when you know too well it's about a book you are writing going down like ground glass.

She looks at you out the corner of her eye, says nothing.

Your older son gets up from his lawn chair, and moves even farther away with his friend, and you look at him, too. He's got on sunglasses, a ball cap on backward. He's embarrassed by you, you know.

You would have been, too, were you him.

But the book is dying. It is dying.

You yell, even louder, "Let's GO! Get in the GAME!" and feel your hands in fists on the arms of the lawn chair.

This time your younger son looks over his shoulder, though far downfield, and his eyes meet yours. Then, quickly, they dart away, to others on the sidelines, then to the ground, his back fully to you now, him running and running.

"He's always just hanging back like that," you say to your wife, quieter but, you only now realize, with your teeth clenched. "It's like he's always just watching what's going on." You know your words as you speak them are one more attempt to give your anger, your resentment a clear conscience: you're yelling because of your kid. Not because of you.

And now your wife stands, picks up her lawn chair, moves away, settles her chair a good fifty feet from you.

This is no signal to you of the embarrassment you are. It is nothing cryptic you are meant to decipher. It is her truth and yours both, big and dumb: you are a fool.

And it is because of a book. A stupid book. *There are more important things,* she is shouting to you in settling her lawn chair that far from you. There are more important things than a book.

You are here in your chair, alone with yourself. And the corpse of your book propped beside you.

You look off to the right, for no good reason but that it's away from those you have embarrassed, and those who know you for the fool you are.

And see there near the sideline, almost to the corner of the field, a blond kid, down on one knee on the sideline, his back to you. He's maybe ten yards away, the sun falling across the field to give his blond hair an extra shimmer to it, turning it almost white.

He's talking to himself, you hear, his voice quiet but there, just there. He's got on a black T-shirt, cargo shorts, skateboard shoes, and though his back is to you, you can see he has in one hand a plastic yellow baseball bat, in the other a plastic Day-Glo orange squirt gun.

He's holding them oddly, you can see, the bat by the thick end, where the ball makes contact, the handle up and perpendicular to the ground, like a flagstaff with no flag; the squirt gun he holds delicately, thumb and first finger at the bottom of the grip, as though it might be too hot.

He's still talking, and you can see the gun and bat moving a little, first the gun, his hand shaking it in sync, you hear, with his words, then the bat, the movement small, like the sound of his voice coming to you across the grass, and over the shouts of players at the far end of the field. Then the gun shakes again, and you see too by the movement of his head that he looks at the gun when he moves it and talks, and looks as well at the bat when he moves it and talks.

What is he doing?

Then he turns, rolls toward you from the knee he is on to sitting flat on the ground. He's facing you now, still holding the bat and gun in this odd way, and you see, now, now, he is a Down syndrome boy: almond eyes, thick neck, his mouth open.

He speaks again, looks at the bat, moving it with his words, and you only now realize he is speaking for the bat, that the bat itself is talking, this boy supplying the words, and then the gun answers the bat.

They are talking one to the other: a yellow bat, a Day-Glo squirt gun.

The boy is about your younger son's age, you see, and see too the shimmer of late afternoon sunlight in his hair the same as a few moments before, when his back was to you, and you hadn't known. You hadn't known.

You look at him. Still they talk one to the other, the words nothing you can make out, but there is something beautiful and profound in what you see. Something right and simple and true, and just past your understanding.

It's a kind of peace you see, and can't understand, this moment.

I wrote a book about that, you think. I wrote a book about a Down syndrome person, my aunt, and her mother. My grandmother, you think.

That was a good book, you think. That one was a gift, given to you without your even asking.

A gift, you think, and you wonder who this boy is with, who his own family is, whom he is a gift to, and just as you wonder this you hear a rise in the crowd.

Parents and children in lawn chairs are growing louder now, clapping, hollering, though nothing as bombastic as what you knew you let out a few minutes before, and you turn to the sound, see your son's team moving and moving before the goal down there, the ball popped to the left and then right, and now you hear from the boy the word "Go," then louder, "Go! GO!" and you look at him, see him turned to that end of the field now too, see the bat and gun held still, this boy back up on one knee and in profile to you. "GO JOHNNY!" he yells, and you know he has a brother out there.

The gun and bat talk to each other again, while the shadows from the far side of the field grow closer to you all, to everyone, and now you know you knew nothing in writing that book. It was a gift, this story of a mother and daughter, but has it made you a better father to your son? Has it made you a better husband to your wife?

The answer, of course, is no, because here you are, chewing out the world around you because a book is going down like ground glass swallowed.

This is when the boy happens to glance up from the dialogue he creates and lives at once, to see you looking at him. Your eyes meet a moment, the talking toys now still, and you say, "Hi." You say it just to be nice to him. You say it because your eyes have met, and he has seen you watching him.

But you say it to try and save yourself.

He looks at you, looks at you, and even before he goes back to the dialogue at hand, his friends these toys, you know he won't say a thing.

You are a stranger.

You look beside you. There is no corpse of a book here, not anywhere around. Your wife is gone too, her to your left and away from you, your older son even farther away. And there is your younger son, out on the field and running away from you as best he can. Your son, a teammate to this boy's brother.

There is, you know, only you here with you, and though you wish it were possible, pray it might be possible, there is no way for you to stand and lift your lawn chair and walk fifty feet away from you.

Which is what you want to do. To be away from you, here.

Because you have been blessed.

You have been blessed.

You have been blessed.

o

You have everything to learn.

This will be what keeps you. What points you toward humility: knowing how very little you know, how very far you have to go. As far now, in the second person and once it's all over, as on an afternoon soccer field, shadows growing long.

I know nothing. I know I know nothing.

I have been blessed.

for Jim Ferry

Acknowledgments

• •

Most of the essays in this book were given as lectures at Vermont College while I was on the faculty of the M.F.A. program, and I want to thank the students there who were willing to listen to me pontificate on how I know nothing. Especially helpful in shaping these pieces was my good and dear and wise friend David Jauss, whose counsel time and again proved immeasurably valuable. Mark Cox and Robin Hemley were also generous in their advice, and remain extraordinary friends. I'd also like to thank my editor, Bruce Tracy, for making me sit down and write that piece about rejection, an essay I only now realize was absolutely necessary in telling the truth about what it means to be a writer. Thanks also and always go to my agent, Marian Young, who saw something in an unfinished novel I sent her twenty years ago, and who remains an encourager and supporter—my big sister—these many years and many books later.

And finally, my thanks go to Melanie, whose faith in me has been the bedrock of my writing life. I have been blessed beyond measure by her presence.

AUTHOR'S NOTE

• •

The author would like to thank the editors and publishers of the following magazines, in which these essays originally appeared:

"Genesis" in *Brevity*
"Before We Get Started" in *The Writer's Chronicle*
"Why Write, Anyway?" in *Poets & Writers*
"Toward a Definition of Creative Nonfiction" and "Toward Humility" in *Fourth Genre*
"Against Technique" in *Creative Nonfiction*
"The Ironic Stance and the Law of Diminishing Returns" in *Image: A Journal of the Arts and Religion*
"The Most Fragile Book" in *The Raleigh News and Observer*

"Toward a Definition of Creative Nonfiction" also appeared in *Fourth Genre: Contemporary Writers of/on Creative Nonfiction.*
"The Ironic Stance and the Law of Diminishing Returns" also appeard in the anthology *Best Spiritual Writing 2002.*

Author's Note

"The Most Fragile Book" also appeared in *The Book I Read: Writers and Their Adventures as Readers*.

"Toward Humility" also appeared in *The Utne Reader*, *Pushcart Prize XXV*, *Best Essays from the Pushcart Prize*, and *Best Spiritual Writing 2001*.

Selected Bibliography

Jacques Barzun. *From Dawn to Decadence: 500 Years of Western Cultural Life, 1500 to the Present*. New York: Perennial, 2001.

Charles Baxter. *Burning Down the House*. St. Paul: Graywolf Press, 1998.

Raymond Carver. *Fires: Essays, Poems, Stories*. New York: Vintage, 1989.

John Gardner. *The Art of Fiction: Notes on Craft for Young Writers*. New York: Alfred A. Knopf, 1984.

———. *On Becoming a Novelist*. New York: W. W. Norton, 1983.

———. *On Moral Fiction*. New York: Basic Books, 1979.

Richard Hugo. *The Triggering Town: Lectures and Essays on Poetry and Writing*. New York: W. W. Norton, 1979.

Henry James. *The Art of the Novel*. Introduction by Richard P. Blackmur. New York: Scribner's, 1962.

Phillip Lopate, ed. *The Art of the Personal Essay: An Anthology from the Classical Era to the Present*. New York: Anchor Books, 1994.

William Maxwell. *The Outermost Dream: Literary Sketches*. St. Paul: Graywolf Press, 1997.

Michel de Montaigne. *The Complete Essays of Montaigne*, translated by Donald M. Frame. Palo Alto, Calif.: Stanford University Press, 1958.

Flannery O'Connor. *The Habit of Being: Letters of Flannery O'Connor*, edited by Sally Fitzgerald. New York: Farrar, Straus and Giroux, 1979.

————. *Mystery and Manners: Occasional Prose*. New York: Farrar, Straus and Giroux, 1969.

Jedediah Purdy. *For Common Things: Irony, Trust and Commitment in America Today*. New York: Vintage, 2000.

John Steinbeck. *Working Days: The Journals of The Grapes of Wrath*, edited by Robert Demott. New York: Viking, 1989.

Jerome Stern. *Making Shapely Fiction*. New York: W. W. Norton, 1991.

William Strunk, Jr., and E. B. White. *The Elements of Style*. 4th ed. Needham Heights, Mass.: Allyn & Bacon, 2000.

Brenda Ueland. *If You Want to Write: A Book About Art, Independence and Spirit*. St. Paul: Graywolf Press, 1997.

Vincent van Gogh. *Dear Theo: The Autobiography of Vincent van Gogh*, edited by Irving Stone and Jean Stone. New York: Plume, 1995.

Eudora Welty. *One Writer's Beginnings*. New York: Warner Books, 1985.

E. B. White. *Letters of E. B. White*, edited by Dorothy Lobrano Guth. New York: HarperCollins, 1989.

ABOUT THE AUTHOR

BRET LOTT is the author of the novels *A Song I Knew by Heart, Jewel* (an Oprah's Book Club selection in 1999), *Reed's Beach, A Stranger's House, The Man Who Owned Vermont,* and *The Hunt Club;* the story collections *A Dream of Old Leaves* and *How to Get Home;* and the memoir *Fathers, Sons, and Brothers.* From 1986 to 2004 he was writer in residence and professor of English at the College of Charleston in Charleston, South Carolina; he was also a professor in the low-residency M.F.A. program at Vermont College from 1994 to 2003. He and his wife now live in Baton Rouge, Louisiana, where he is editor of *The Southern Review* and professor of English at Louisiana State University.

ABOUT THE TYPE

The text of this book was set in a digitized version of Figural, a typeface originally designed in 1940 by the Czech calligrapher and book designer Oldřich Menhart. It is an expressionistic face, echoing the forms of rough, pen-made letters.